Sensational Seas of

SABAH

Sensational Seas of SABAH

Words & Photography
Jason Isley, Gilbert Woolley & Christian Loader

scubazoo

Publications

MANAGING EDITOR	*Jason Isley*
PROJECT EDITOR	*Gilbert Woolley*
ART EDITOR	*Karen Chao*
TEXT EDITOR	*Matthew Oldfield*
SALES/MARKETING	*Simon Christopher*
ONLINE VIDEO BY	*Simon Enderby*
	Roger Munns
	Chris Tan
	Sam Lewis
	Christian Loader
FOOTAGE RESEARCH	*Cara Morrison*
	Lou Love
EDITING	*Damian Antochewicz*

TEXT AND IMAGES
Copyright © Scubazoo Images Sdn. Bhd.
www.scubazoo.com

First published 2013
Sensational Seas of Sabah by
Scubazoo Images Sdn. Bhd.
ISBN 978-967-10528-2-2

Printed by
Percetakan Nasional Malaysia Berhad (PNMB),
Jalan Chan Sow Lin, 50554 Kuala Lumpur.
www. printnasional.com.my

Front cover: Chevron Barracuda (*Sphyraena qenie*). Pulau Sipadan.

Inside front cover: Coral reef at Pulau Mantabuan, with Pulau
Bohey Dulang and Pulau Gaya in the background.

Inside back cover: Chevron Barracuda (*Sphyraena qenie*)
over the shallow reef. Pulau Sipadan.

Page 2: A White-tip Reef Shark (*Trianodon obesus*) followed by
Big-eye Trevally (*Caranx sexfasciatus*). Pulau Sipadan.

Page 4 & 5: A large, graceful Manta Ray (*Manta alfredi*) glides
through the ocean. Layang Layang.

contents

Foreword

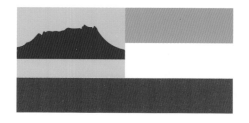

MESSAGE FROM THE RIGHT HONOURABLE CHIEF MINISTER OF SABAH

I am honoured to pen a few words for this publication, which I believe will go a long way in further promoting Sabah's natural treasures, and I congratulate everyone who played a role in putting this book together.

Part of Sabah's great strength lies in the richness of her natural resources – the forests, rivers and seas lay claim to some of the highest recorded levels of biodiversity on our planet. Surrounded by three seas, the South China, Sulu and Celebes, Sabah's waters contain a rich underwater realm, offering some of the world's best diving. From shallow fringing reefs to vast meadows of seagrass and deep oceanic drop-offs, the diversity of habitats around Sabah's coastline and surrounding islands offer even the most well-travelled divers and snorkellers everything they could wish for.

The bountiful seas are a major attraction for visiting tourists and locals to enjoy, yet also provide an invaluable resource for many people living along the coastline. Sabah has long recognised the importance of maintaining the richness of the seas surrounding its coastline for this very reason. Efforts to conserve fish stocks and remove the threat of illegal fishing techniques have been part of government policy for many years.

The Government is committed towards efforts to protect our seas and terrestrial landscapes, as reflected in development plans, including the Sabah Development Corridor (SDC) blueprint. We acknowledge the importance of conserving our biodiversity, and we are always open to hearing the views of various stakeholders in ensuring that our natural heritage is not compromised in the long run. I assure you that Sabah takes great pride in our diverse natural treasures.

The images within this book help illustrate the amazing biodiversity many people will never get to experience first-hand. It is vital that we take pride in protecting and preserving these environmental and economic assets for future generations.

Kudos on a job well done.

Datuk Seri Panglima Musa Hj Aman,
Chief Minister of Sabah, Malaysia.

Preface

MESSAGE FROM MINISTER OF TOURISM, CULTURE AND ENVIRONMENT, SABAH

For many years Sabah has been a scuba diving mecca, with the focus firmly on the tiny oceanic island of Sipadan. A magnet for experienced divers from around the world, Sipadan's fame is well deserved and visitors are rewarded for their trip by drifting through vast schools of trevally and barracuda, coming face-to-face with incredibly friendly turtles and watching enthralled as sharks circle in the blue. With steps taken by the government in 2004 to ensure Sipadan's continued protection it seems that divers will enjoy its vibrant reef system for many years to come.

While Sipadan has historically claimed the spotlight, this book aims to showcase other, perhaps lesser-known, locations found in Sabah's seas, and the abundant marine life found there. Layang Layang plays host to a shiver of Hammerhead Sharks while beautiful, bizarre critters dwell amongst the shallow reefs of Mabul and the Semporna Strait. Rare and wonderful species like the Weedy Scorpionfish and even the largest fish of them all, the Whale Shark, can be encountered a mere fifteen minutes by boat from Sabah's capital Kota Kinabalu – a location better known until now for scuba diving courses and first-time snorkelling.

With their incredible photographs and in-depth knowledge, Scubazoo hope to share these lesser-known treasures and encourage tourists and local divers alike to explore more of Sabah's coastline. Under threat from climate change, acidification, commercial fishing and coastal development the world's coral reefs face an uncertain future. By showcasing the entire coastline of Sabah I hope Sabahans and indeed all Malaysians will continue to be proud guardians of the life found within Sabah's Sensational Seas.

Datuk Masidi Manjun
The Honourable Minister of Tourism and Environmental Development
Sabah, Malaysia

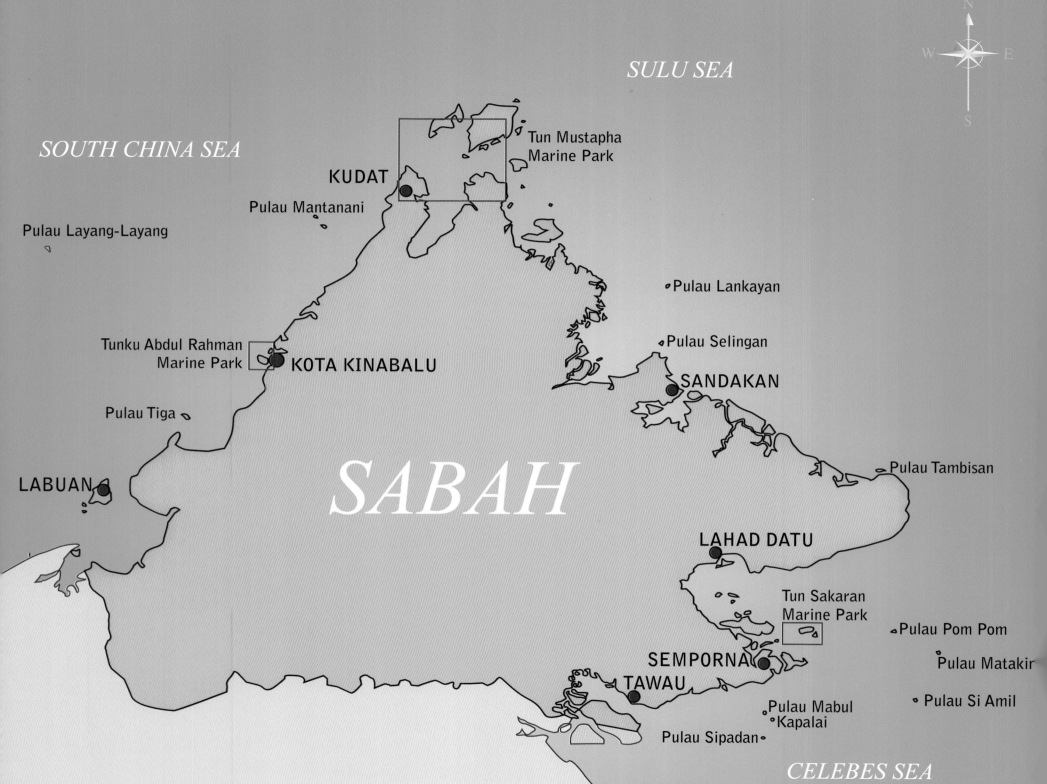

Introduction

The Malaysian state of Sabah straddles the northern tip of one of the world's largest islands – Borneo. With its ancient rainforests, rugged, granite-peaked mountains, idyllic lagoons and pristine beaches, it encapsulates the very best of this ancient island. Sabah lies at the heart of the 'Coral Triangle' and is home to some of the world's greatest marine biodiversity; it is this hidden beauty below the surface of the sea that draws divers and snorkellers from around the world. Sabah's tourism industry has become a highly valuable source of income for the state and at any time of the year, visitors from Asia, Europe and America can be seen enjoying the aquatic natural wonders.

Three different seas surround Sabah: the South China Sea to the west, the Sulu Sea to the north and the Celebes Sea to the east. The South China Sea can be explored from Sabah's capital city, Kota Kinabalu, and includes the Tunku Abdul Rahman Marine Park, Pulau Tiga to the south and the coral atoll of Layang Layang 300km to the west. Further north are Pulau Mantanani and Usukan Bay, home to a number of wrecks sunk during World War 2. The Sulu Sea is home to the proposed Tun Mustapha Marine Park and the remote island of Pulau Lankayan. To the east, the Celebes Sea has many tropical islands dotted along the coastline, including those that make up the Tun Sakaran Marine Park to the north of Semporna. This small town is also the gateway for many other extraordinary dive locations including Pulau Mataking, Pulau Mabul, Kapalai and, of course, the world famous island of Sipadan.

Sabah's coastline has its fair share of exquisite beaches but much is covered by large stretches of mangrove forests, an important habitat that helps to protect the coastline from the action of wind and waves and acts as a nursery for many fish found on the coral reefs. With such a diverse range of islands and locations it is no surprise that the underwater environment found below the surface of these seas is so rich and abundant with life.

▶ Tourist snorkellers exploring one of Sabah's many stunning coral reefs. Pulau Pom Pom.

The 'Coral Triangle' is considered the global epicentre of marine biodiversity. The entire area represents one of the richest marine habitats in the world and an estimated 3,000 different species of fish, more than 500 reef-building coral species and more than 30% of the world's coral reefs can be found here. Understandably, Sabah – lying at the heart of this extraordinary region – can claim to have some of the highest marine biodiversity on the planet.

Among the marine treasures frequently encountered in Sabah's waters are rare or endangered reptiles such as Green and Hawksbill Turtles, magnificent Napoleon Wrasse, Giant Clams, different species of sharks and dense schools of barracuda and trevally. In fact, at locations such as Sipadan, it's not uncommon to find yourself surrounded by many of these creatures all at once. Sipadan and the west coast atoll of Layang Layang are also famous for occasional sightings of schools of Hammerhead Sharks and frequent encounters with huge schools of Bumphead Parrotfish. Other large pelagics, such as Manta and Devils Rays, are often seen as they visit the reefs for cleaning or feeding, and even Mola Mola have been encountered. The largest fish of them all, the Whale Shark, occasionally visits Sipadan, Palau Mabul and Layang Layang, however it's the regular annual visits to Tunku Abdul Rahman Marine Park, just opposite Kota Kinabalu that makes for some very special encounters for dive students completing their diving courses.

As well as these larger inhabitants, Sabah offers 'muck diving' enthusiasts such rarities as the Mimic Octopus, Flamboyant Cuttlefish, Weedy Scorpionfish, seahorses and different frogfish. Pulau Mabul, Kapalai and Pulau Mataking all have extensive shallow, sandy seabeds; perfect places to explore and hunt for these bizarre 'critters'. House reefs and jetties have always been known as great locations for dives, searching for and photographing the resident jawfish, Mandarinfish, Pygmy Seahorses and eels. And the more recent exploration of the Semporna Strait as a dive location has uncovered what is possibly the best muck diving in Sabah. Within a small area many rare creatures like the Flamboyant Cuttlefish, Lembeh Seadragon, Picturesque Dragonet and Halimeda Ghost Pipefish can all be found.

Regardless of the type of diving you prefer, or creatures you hope to encounter, Sabah has something in store for everyone and in fact, it is best to combine a few different locations during a single trip to make the most of what Sabah has to offer.

◀ Fascinating 'critters' such as this tiny Pygmy Seahorse (*Hippocampus bargibanti*) can be found all around Sabah.

▶ Pulau Sipadan is undoubtedly one of Malaysia's national treasures, where the profusion of biodiversity has to be seen to be believed. Big-eye Trevally (*Caranx sexfasciatus*) and Bluestreak Fusiliers (*Pterocaesio tile*) gather in large schools over a shallow reef, wary of predatory Giant Trevally (*Caranx ignobilis*) and White-tip Reef Sharks (*Triaenodon obesus*).

▲ A Painted Terrapin (*Callagur borneoensis*) takes a breath of air amongst the roots of mangrove trees. Tuaran, West Sabah.

The dazzling colours and vibrant inhabitants of the coral reefs may be the biggest attraction for visiting divers, however Sabah is also blessed with large areas of mangrove forests and vast beds of seagrass. As well as being interesting dive locations, these areas also have a much more important role to play in the underwater environment.

The mangrove forests that cling to the coastline of the mainland and islands like Pulau Tiga, Pulau Gaya and Pulau Banggi act as an important barrier between land and sea, protecting the land from erosion and the sea from plumes of sediment washed out by the rivers. The roots of the mangrove trees also create a labyrinth of dark passages that provide protection for many fish and act as an underwater nursery for juveniles of species found on nearby reefs. These young fish develop amongst the mangroves in safety, assuming they can escape the attention of young sharks that also use the same root system for both protection and as their hunting grounds.

In the sunlit, shallow seas around Sabah, seagrass beds are found in abundance. Like mangrove forests, these play an important role by helping to stabilize the shifting sands of the seabed. The vast grassy plains may, at first glance, appear to be devoid of life but they are host to many strange and wonderful creatures like seahorses, pipefish and bizarre, highly camouflaged Ambon Scorpionfish. Seagrass beds are also important for larger creatures; Green Turtles can be seen in the shallow waters of Sipadan at high tide, feeding on the seagrass, whilst Dugongs carve out long trails as they graze like underwater cows.

▲ This rare Ambon Scorpionfish (*Pteroidichthys amboinensis*) uses camouflage to hide amongst the seagrass. Pulau Si Amil.

▶ Over 350 species of coral thrive in the pristine, shallow waters around Sabah – which is home to more than 75% of Malaysia's coral reefs. Pulau Timba Timba.

Known as the 'rainforests of the sea', coral reefs are without doubt the world's most biologically diverse marine ecosystems. Sabah lies within the 'Coral Triangle' – the area of the world's oceans recognized by scientists as being the centre of global marine biodiversity – and as such, the reefs around Sabah are home to a huge number of different species. Around the islands and along the coastline, an estimated 500+ species of coral provide food and shelter to fish and invertebrates, as well as protecting the shorelines from erosion.

There are three main types of coral reefs – fringing reefs, barrier reefs and atolls –– and Sabah plays host to all three. The majority around Sabah are fringing reefs however Layang Layang in the South China Sea is a perfect example of an atoll, with its ring-shaped reef enclosing a central lagoon. Running along the east coast, in the Celebes Sea, is the Sipadan Barrier Reef, which runs for more than 95km and is composed of 15 individual reefs and 11 islands, including Pulau Si Amil, Pulau Timba Timba, Pulau Bohayan and Pulau Ligitan.

The seas surrounding Sabah are not simply playgrounds for visiting tourists and divers, nor a museum or living laboratory for scientists. Instead, both the reefs and open ocean play a vitally important role as a source of food and income for the people that live along the coastline.

▲ A Reef Octopus (*Octopus cyanea*) sustainably caught by an old fisherman. The traditional and ingenious method used here, involved towing a weighted, fake 'bait' octopus (made of a polystyrene body with hooks, and arms made of fabric) slowly above the reef. The live octopus, tricked into thinking it has a potential mate, swims to the bait and gets hooked. Pulau Kalapuan.

▲ Stilt houses built over a shallow seagrass bed. Pulau Bohey Dulang.

These communities have relied on the sea as their main source of protein for generations and have handed down ingenious ways of catching different marine creatures. When staying on the islands you will witness children and families collecting sea urchins, sea cucumbers and other reef dwelling creatures at low tide, but it's underwater where the more creative techniques are utilised. The Bajau fishermen on the east coast make fake octopus from material and rubber and use them to lure real octopus from their holes. Other fishermen have become experts at the art of free-diving, swimming down to 20m on a single breath, speargun in hand, and then walking over the reef in search of their unsuspecting victims.

Today, these traditional fishermen have to work alongside large commercial vessels – employing modern fishing techniques with huge drag nets – and compete for the same, dwindling numbers of fish. Some communities have now turned to other commercial ventures such as seaweed and pearl farming, bringing in a steady income whilst helping to conserve Sabah's precious natural resources.

▶ A local spearfisherman hunting for his family's next meal in the waters off the east coast of Semporna.

South China Sea

▲ Aerial view of the Southern beach along Pulau Tiga.

Pulau Tiga

Pulau Tiga was formed just over a century ago when an earthquake, with its epicentre many kilometres away in the Philippines, triggered a volcanic eruption 20km off the west coast of Sabah – the result of which was the birth of a new island. Thankfully no further tremors have occurred in recent history and the only reminder of the island's turbulent creation is a 'volcano' still bubbling hot mud in the centre of the island. Pulau Tiga has matured beautifully and now boasts long sandy beaches and sheltered lagoons, although the many large Monitor Lizards that patrol the beaches can give the island a distinctly prehistoric feel.

Below the surface of the sea, the reefs around Pulau Tiga appear to be blanketed with colour as extensive patches of soft corals in orange, yellow, purple and red stretch across the sea floor. Massive hard coral outcrops dot the seabed, providing shelter for large numbers of schooling fish and, on closer inspection, a wide variety of critters that shelter within. This nutrient-rich sea is both home and breeding ground for a huge number of different species that all thrive under the protection offered by the National Park centred around this uninhabited island.

◀ A Water Monitor Lizard (*Varanus salvator*) swimming on the surface.

◀◀ Pulau Kalampunian Damit (or Snake Island) with Pulau Tiga in the background.

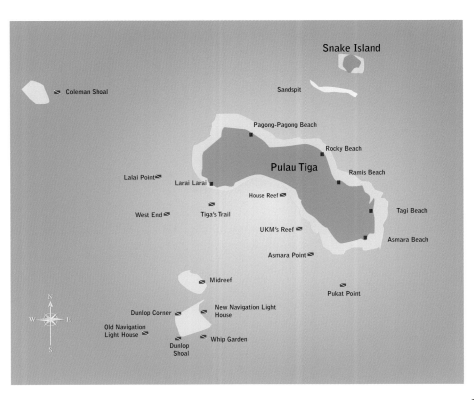

▲ Banded Sea Snake (*Laticauda colubrina*).

The Banded Sea Snake will dive down to the seabed for up to 1 hour on a single breath, searching in crevices where it preys on small fish and eels. Whilst probing these crevices with its head and thus unable to detect approaching threats, it can fool potential predators to believe that its tails is actually its head, based on both colouration and tail movements. Although these snakes have extremely venomous rear fangs to quickly immobilize prey before being swallowed, with their small mouths and relatively docile nature they are very little actual threat to scuba divers or snorkelers.

▲ Water Monitor Lizards (*Varanus salvator*) are excellent swimmers and use the raised fin on their tails to power and steer through the water.

◀ Soft coral covering the reef.

▶ A variety of sedentary invertebrates encrust the reef, including soft coral, sea fans and sponges.

❝ The rich colours of Sabah's reefs amaze me every time I slowly descend below the surface. The blue and green hues of the reef below give way to a kaleidoscope of vibrant colours as the abundant sponges and corals get closer. ❞

◀ Divers exploring crevices in a coral 'bommie'.

◀ The 'bommie' provides shelter for shrimps, crabs, and small reef fish.

▶ A school of Yellowtail Barracuda (*Sphyraena flavicauda*).

Commensal Sea Star Shrimp
(*Periclimenes soror*).

◄ A Common Seahorse (*Hippocamp taeniopterus*) clings to a clump of soft coral with its prehensile tail.

▲ Aerial view of the beach at Pulau Sapi.

Tunku Abdul Rahman Marine Park

Covering an area of approximately 50km², Tunku Abdul Rahman Marine Park is one of the most accessible dive locations in Sabah, situated just 15 minutes by boat from the state's capital city, Kota Kinabalu. The park comprises 5 islands – Pulau Gaya, Sapi, Manukan, Mamutik and Sulug, with well over 30 dive sites divided between the islands.

For a location so close to a major city, the reefs within TARP still have surprisingly good coral cover and a high biodiversity, with an estimated 364 different fish species living within TARP's boundaries. One of the reasons for this high biodiversity is that the park encompasses a wide range of habitats – you can be 'muck' diving with a Blue-ringed Octopus on your first dive of the day, exploring colourful reefs with passing Black-tip Reef Sharks on the second and interacting with turtles and cuttlefish on one of the islands' house reefs on the final dive. And from November to February, plankton blooms attract both krill and any passing Whale Sharks. An underwater encounter with one of these colossal animals, particular when they suddenly emerge out of the gloom created by such dense clouds of krill, is simply unforgettable.

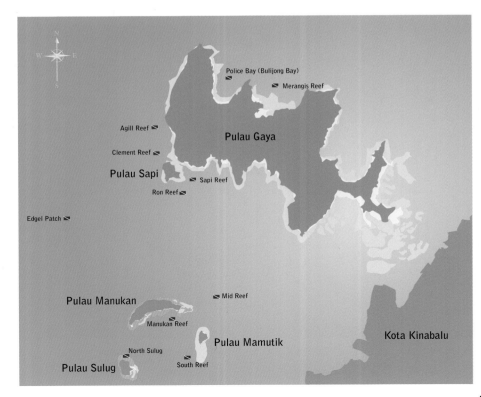

◀ Whale Shark (*Rhincodon typus*) feeding on krill. Pulau Sapi.

▲ A school of Big-eye Snapper (*Lutjanus lutjanus*) & sponges. Pulau Sulug.

▲ A Common Lionfish (*Pterois volitans*) hunting Glassfish (*Parapriacanthus sp.*). Pulau Sulug.

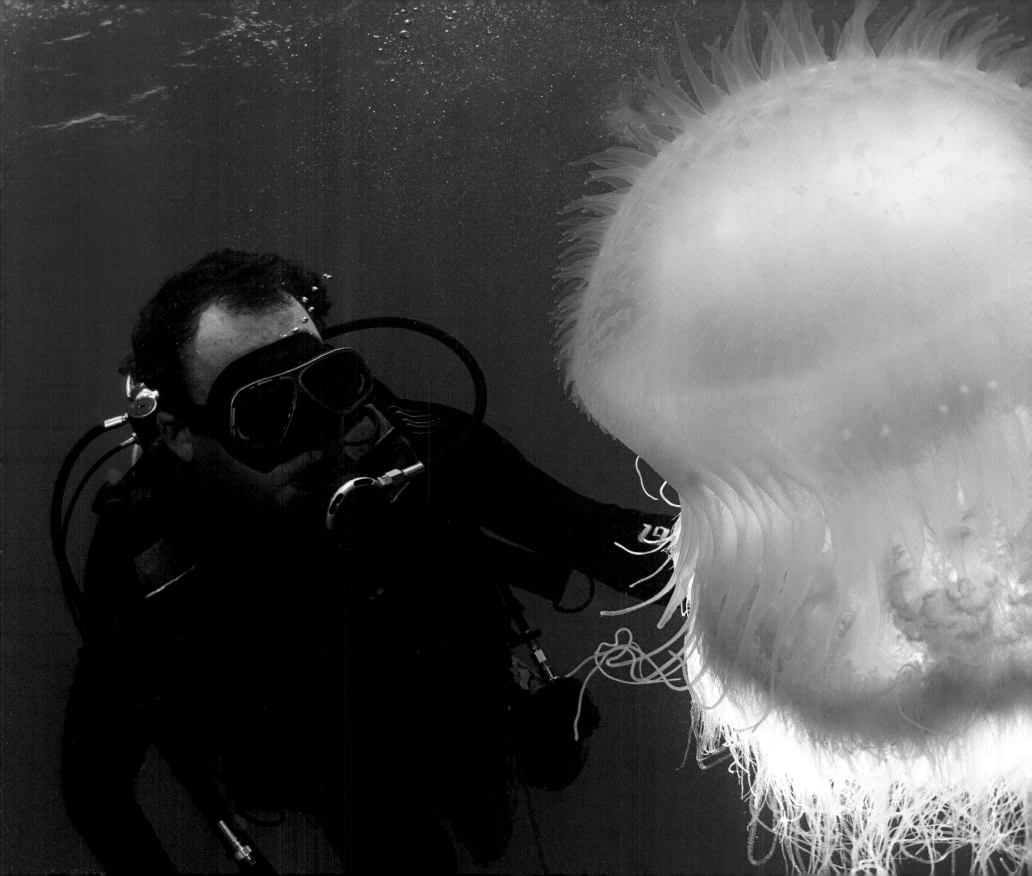

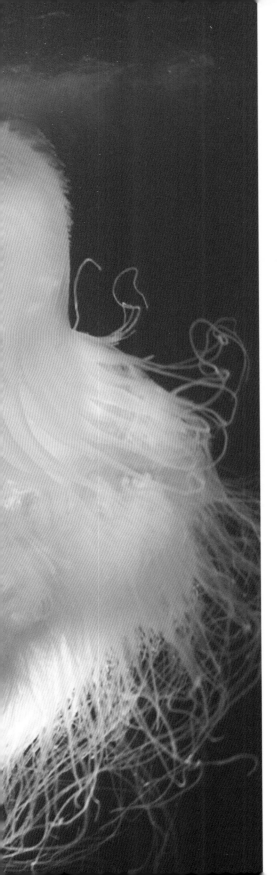

Large jellyfish drift across vast oceans, feeding on plankton and small fish caught in their deadly, stinging tentacles. Rising sea temperatures caused by climate change are known to contribute to jellyfish blooms, as many species are better able to survive in warmer water.

▲ Crab hiding amongst the body of the jellyfish. Pulau Sapi.

◄ A diver & jellyfish. Pulau Sapi.

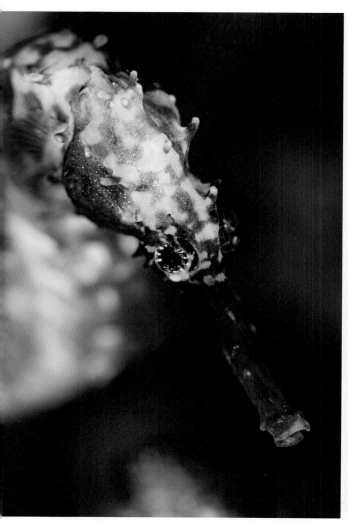

▲ Tiger-tail Seahorse (*Hippocampus comes*). Pulau Sapi.

▲ Juvenile Half-spined Seahorse (*Hippocampus semispinosus*). Pulau Sulug.

▲ Tiger-tail Seahorse (*Hippocampus comes*). Pulau Sulug.

Seahorses are found in tropical and temperate waters throughout the world. The 40+ species of seahorse come in many colours and although they may look docile, they are predators and feed on small shrimps by sucking them up with their long snouts.

An Ornate Ghost
Pipefish (*Solenostomus
paradoxus)* perfectly
camouflaged amongst
the fronds of a feather
star. Pulau Mamutik.

▲ Mid-ring Blue-ringed Octopus (*Hapalochlaena sp*). Pulau Sapi.

Octopus can often be found by searching the sandy seabeds around Sabah. These highly intelligent invertebrates are masters of camouflage, using specialized skin cells to change the colour and pattern of their skin to match their environment, whether it be sand, rock, or algae. They can also utilise this skill to flash warning signs of their toxicity to potential predators.

▲ The eyes of a Wunderpus Octopus (*Wunderpus photogenicus*). Pulau Sapi.

▲ A Mimic Octopus (*Thaumoctopus mimicus*) peers out from its burrow. Pulau Sapi.

I have probably dived Sapi over one hundred times but I still manage to be amazed at the new critters that can be found there. We were lucky enough to spot a very rare Marble-mouth Frogfish which we hadn't seen before, and on closer inspection we saw it had eggs attached to the side of its body. We returned to watch it over several days as the eggs developed and eventually perfectly formed baby frogfish hatched and were washed away in the current.

▶ The eggs of the Marble-mouth Frogfish (*Lophiocharon lithinostomus*). Pulau Sapi.

◀ A rare, male Marble-mouth Frogfish (*Lophiocharon lithinostomus*) with a cluster of eggs attached to the side of its body. Pulau Sapi.

▶ A Weedy Scorpionfish (*Rhinopias frondosa*) is well camouflaged amongst algae on the seabed, and is a highly prized find for lucky divers. Pulau Sulug.

◀ A pair of Coleman's Shrimp (*Periclimenes colemani*) living safely amongst the protective spines of a sea urchin. Mid Reef.

▶ A Spotted Moray Eel (*Gymnothorax isingteena*) hiding in a reef crevice. Pulau Sulug.

▲ Pulau Mantanani Kecil.

Pulau Mantanani & Usukan Bay

Famous for its white, sandy beaches and crystal clear blue water, Pulau Mantanani, located just an hour's boat ride away from Kuala Abai, 80km north of Kota Kinabalu, is fast becoming a popular tourist destination. Most of the diving takes place around the three islands, Mantanani Besar, Kecil and Lungisan, while three, large Japanese wrecks from World War II are located nearby in Usukan Bay.

Around the main island, patches of diverse hard corals form extensive reefs interspersed with sandy patches that can be explored at leisure in the gentle currents and clear water. Closer to the small islands it can be more thrilling to dive amongst the rocky outcrops and caves, where currents are often less predictable. Further away from Mantanani – and reserved for the real thrill seeker – the wrecks offer some deeper diving on sites that have become home to a vast array of marine life. The wrecks have good invertebrate cover, huge fish populations and, on occasion, larger sharks and rays, which when combined with the historic interest of these remarkably intact ships make for some fascinating dives.

◀ The jetty at Pulau Mantanani Kecil provides shelter for this school of Slender Silversides (*Hypoatherina barnesi*).

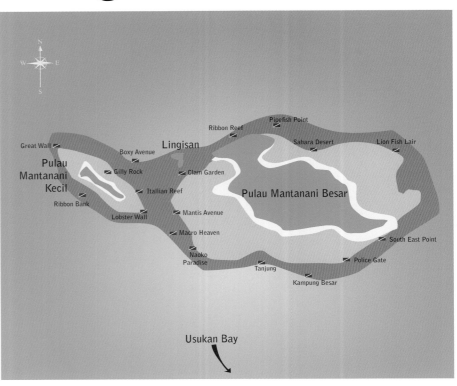

43

Anemonefish have a mucus coating which protects them from the stinging tentacles of the sea anemone it lives on, therefore safe from predators. Anemonefish feed on algae, plankton, and small invertebrates and parasites that could potentially harm the sea anemone, while the fecal matter from the anemonefish provides nutrients for the sea anemone.

◄ False Clown Anemonefish (*Amphiprion ocellaris*) in Magnificent Sea Anemone (*Hecteractis magnifica*). Pulau Mantanani Besar.

▲ Healthy coral reef. Sabah contains more than 75% of all Malaysian reefs. Pulau Mantanani Besar

Colourful reef fish look dazzling to the human eye, but underwater their vibrant colours and patterns can actually help them to blend into their colourful surroundings, confusing would-be predators. In some species, bright colours could advertise their toxic nature to ward off predators, while for other species they are a way of attracting a mate.

▶ Checkerboard Wrasse (*Halichoeres hortulanus*). Pulau Mantanani Besar.

◀ Bullet-head Parrotfish (*Chlorurus sordidus*). Pulau Mantanani Besar.

▶ A small Pink-eye Goby (*Bryaninops natans*) resting on a coral polyp. Pulau Mantanani Besar.

Soft corals may appear more vulnerable to predators than hard corals with a stony skeleton. However, their tissues consist of needle-like spicules, like the thorns of a rose bush, and contain powerful toxins which make them very distasteful to fish.

◀ Soft coral (*Dendronepthya sp.*) on boulders. Usukan Bay.

▶ A dense school of Glassfish (*Parapriacanthus sp.*) around a sea fan (*Echinogorgia sp.*). Usukan Bay.

Diver over the Rice Bowl Wreck, a Japanese cargo ship sunk during World War II, Usukan Bay.

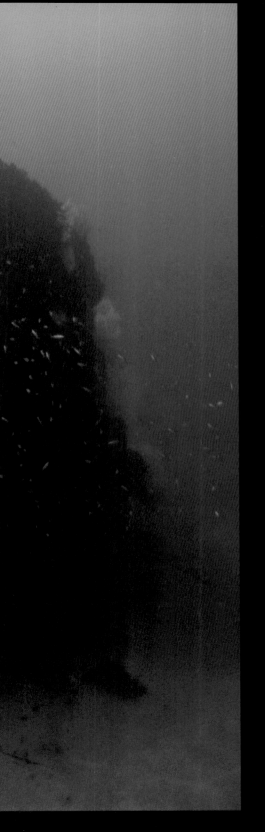

▲ Big-eye Snapper (*Lutjanus lutjanus*) & Crescent Wrasse (*Thalassoma lunare*) on the Rice Bowl Wreck. Usukan Bay.

▲ Diver & Big-eye Snapper (*Lutjanus lutjanus*) on the Rice Bowl Wreck. Usukan Bay.

▲ Bird colony on Layang Layang.

Layang Layang

Malaysia's only atoll, Layang Layang (or Swallow Reef) rises 2,000m from the floor of the South China Sea approximately 300km north-west of Kota Kinabalu. The atoll's almost total isolation means stunning visibility and pristine reefs, along with rich, pelagic marine life. In recent years, Layang Layang has been the site of many special encounters, including with Whale Sharks, Orcas, Melon-headed Whales and even Sperm Whales.

The steep walls of this remote atoll are covered with healthy corals and huge sea fans, spanning up to 3m in width. Green and Hawksbill Turtles are often seen resting or feeding on the reef and even rare 'macro' subjects like Pygmy Seahorses, Ornate Ghost Pipefish and frogfish can be encountered.

However, Layang Layang's fame lies with its pelagics, in particular the Scalloped Hammerheads that can be seen in schools cruising the blue water just off the steep walls. Other regular large fish include Grey Reef Sharks, Leopard Sharks, Marbled Rays, Manta Rays and schools of Devil Rays. If you're lucky, Spinner Dolphins may even escort your dive boat back to the resort – a perfect end to a day.

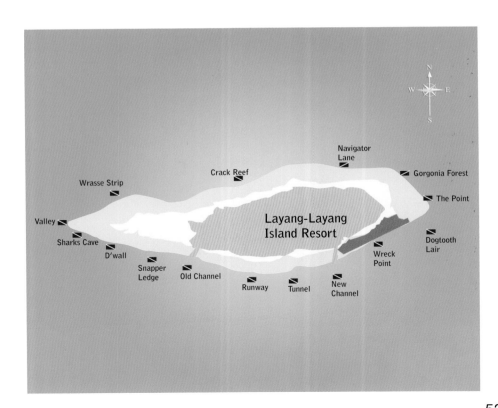

◄ Hawksbill Turtle (*Eretmochelys imbricata*).

▲ Soft coral (*Dendronepthya sp.*).

▲ Whip coral (*Ellisella sp.*).

Gorgonian sea fans are commonly found on steep walls in Sabah, where they grow out across the current and feed on the stream of plankton-rich water flowing past. Sea fans can grow up to 3m in diameter, with thousands of individual polyps able to catch plankton. The branches of sea fans also provide shelter and food for smaller animals such as gobies, hawkfish, shrimps, and the minute and fascinating Pygmy Seahorse.

▶ Gorgonian sea fans (*Subergorgia mollis*).

Many species of fish form schools, providing a better chance of finding a mate, and enhancing foraging success. The 'safety in numbers' hypothesis enables the school a greater chance of detecting predators, while the fish are also less likely to fall victim as it becomes difficult for a predator to single out an individual. The sensory overload created by a swirling, flashing school of silver fish can easily confuse a predator.

▲ A school of Blue-striped Snapper (*Lutjanus kasmira*).

▶ Big-eye Trevally (*Caranx sexfasciatus*).

▼ Pennant Bannerfish (*Heniochus chrysostomus*).

▲ Divers exploring inside Shark's Cave.

▲ A school of Magenta Slender Anthias (*Luzonichthys waitei*) swim into the current.

Fish of all sizes are often seen congregating a 'cleaning stations' on the reef, waiting for their turr to be cleaned by Cleaner Wrasse which rid them o harmful parasites, even swimming into the oper mouths and gill cavities of larger predatory fish Parasite removal is very important for a predator and so Cleaner Wrasse have no fear of being eaten.

△ Spotted Sweetlips (*Plectorhinchus chaetodonoides*) being cleaned by a Blue-streak Cleaner Wrasse (*Labroides dimidiatus*).

◄ Honeycomb Moray Eel (*Gymnothorax favagineus*) being cleaned by a juvenile Blue-streak Cleaner Wrasse (*Labroides dimidiatus*).

► A Common Lionfish (*Pterois volitans*) hovers over the reef.

▲ A diver takes a close look at a Denise's Pygmy Seahorse (*Hippocampus denise*), a rare treat for fortunate divers who find them.

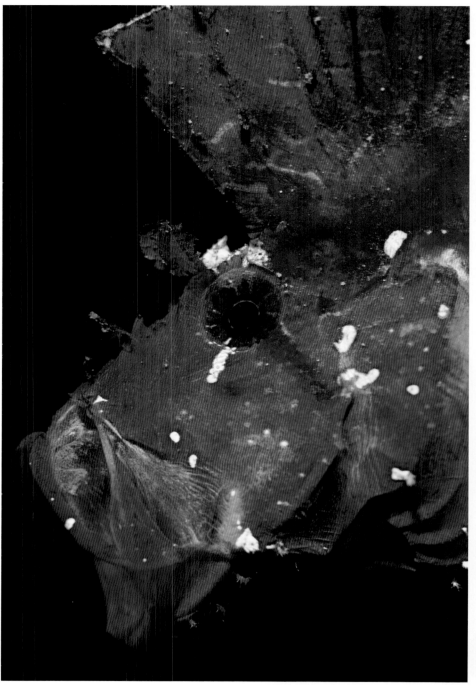

▲ A yawning Leaf Scorpionfish (*Taenianotus triacanthus*).

▶ A Golden Damselfish (*Amblyglyphidodon aureus*) tending its eggs.

▲ A school of Mobula Rays (*Mobula tarapacana*) glide in the blue.

◄ A large Marbled Stingray (*Taeniura meyeni*).

► A pair of Manta Rays (*Manta alfredi*) glide over the reef towards a cleaning station.

" As we cruised along the reef at Wrasse Strip these two Manta Rays appeared like giant birds gliding towards us. Manta Rays are intelligent creatures and I could see an inquisitive flicker in their eyes – were they as curious of me as I was of them? "

▲ A Grey Reef Shark (*Carcharhinus amblyrhynchos*) cruises the reef.

▶ A school of Scalloped Hammerhead Sharks (*Sphyrna lewini*).

Oceanic islands such as Layang Layang serve as meeting places for pelagic species, attracted by the rich food supply. During the daylight hours in deep water, schools of Scalloped Hammerhead Sharks are largely comprised of females actively engaged in social interactions, many of which jockey for the prime social position at the center of the school. At night, these schools break up as individuals move off to hunt for their prey.

The Sulu Sea

▲ Pulau Maliangin Kecil.

Tun Mustapha Marine Park

Situated off the northern tip of Sabah and bordered by the Sulu Sea to the east, the proposed Tun Mustapha Marine Park will become one the largest marine protected areas in Asia, encompassing a total area of approximately 1.1 million hectares. The proposed park covers the coastal areas of Kudat, Kota Marudu and Pitas districts, and will include over 50 islands.

These islands are fringed by dense mangrove forests and healthy reefs abundant in both hard and soft corals and are home to endangered species including sea turtles. There have also been reports of Dugongs and Saltwater Crocodiles from the larger islands of Pulau Banggi and Pulau Balambangan. Numerous small bays and islets around these larger islands are a haven for small critters such as seahorses, frogfish, octopus and nudibranchs.

Unlike other parts of Sabah, this vast area is relatively untouched by the tourism industry and, as the marine park becomes fully established, will offer visiting divers an exciting chance to discover and explore new dive sites.

◀ Pristine hard corals cover the shallow reef. Pulau Maliangin Besar.

◀ ◀ Aerial view of Pulau Lankayan with surrounding reef.

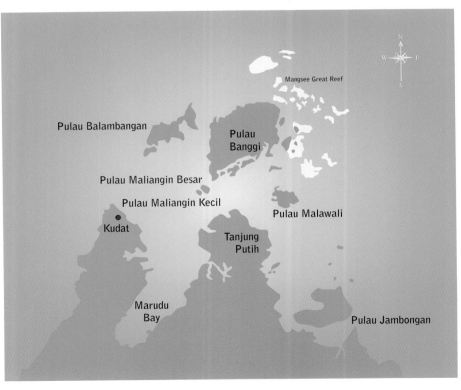

▲ Diver on a coral reef. Pulau Maliangin Kecil.

▲ Hard corals, soft corals and sponges make up a healthy coral reef. Pulau Maliangin Besar.

Coral reefs are the result of millions of years of co-evolution among algae, invertebrates and fish. They occupy less than 1% of the surface area of the world's oceans, but remarkably are home to 25% of all marine fish species – making coral reefs one of Sabah's most valuable assets.

66 *For an underwater photographer the plentiful, tiny marine animals hidden amongst Sabah's reefs are an endless source of delight. As evolution runs wild here in the 'Coral Triangle' countless more species are still being discovered, often with unique colours and camouflage to perfectly match their environment.* 99

◄ A Striped Triplefin (*Helcogramma striatum*) resting on the surface of hard coral. Pulau Maliangin Besar.

▲ A Xenia Shrimp (*Hippolyte commensalis*) mimics the polyps of its host Xenia Soft Coral. Pulau Maliangin Besar.

Unlike larger crabs or Mantis Shrimps which can use their powerful claws to defend themselves from predators, small shrimps must rely on camouflage to perfectly mimic their hosts, such as soft coral.

Many people dive and snorkel over a reef looking at the larger animals, blissfully unaware of the profusion of small and colourful invertebrate species, such as crabs, shrimps and nudibranchs concealed amongst the reef.

▲ A tiny Coral Hermit Crab (*Paguritta harmsi*) burrowed into Porites hard coral. Pulau Maliangin Besar.

◀ A pair of Anna's Chromodoris nudibranchs (*Chromodoris annae*). Pulau Maliangin Besar.

▶ A Military Phidiana nudibranch (*Phidiana militaris*) follows another over the rocky seabed. Pulau Maliangin Besar.

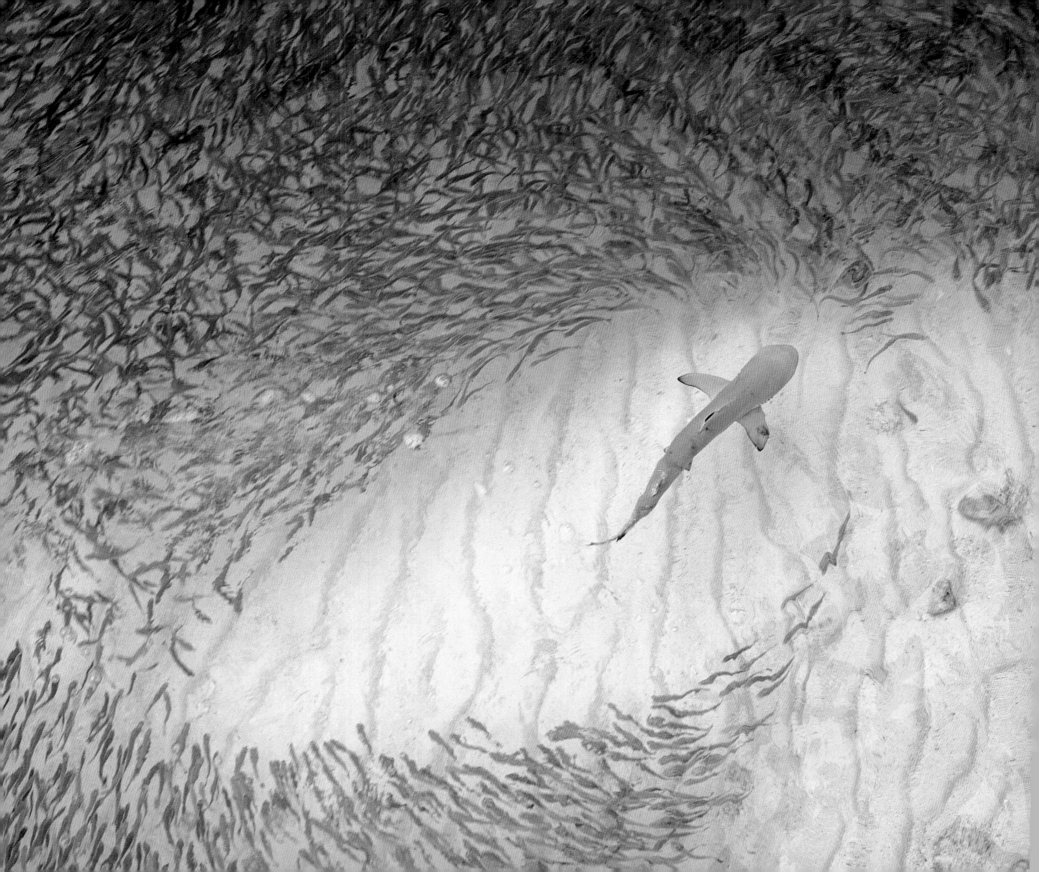

▲ Pulau Lankayan.

Pulau Lankayan

80km north-west of Sandakan is the tiny island paradise of Lankayan. With its perfect sandy beaches, Casuarina trees and total serenity, the island appeals to non-divers and snorkellers, as well as more seasoned divers. Lankayan is part of the Sugud Islands Marine Conservation Area (SIMCA), a private/public sector initiative aimed at protecting and managing the area's marine ecosystem. Soon after the islands were protected, endangered Green and Hawksbill Turtles returned to lay their eggs on the idyllic beaches and subsequently, SIMCA has shown great results over the years.

Lankayan sits on the continental shelf and the surrounding reefs are either fringing or patch reefs, offering some easy and relaxed diving. The macro life is world class, and Lankayan is the only island in Sabah where the charismatic DendriticJawfish can be seen. However, Lankayan also offers regular sightings of Leopard Sharks and Black-tip Reef Sharks.

Closer to shore, the sheltered jetty attracts plenty of marine life, whilst the owners of the resort on the island have also sunk a number of wrecks that are now home to some very large grouper.

◀ A Black-tip Reef Shark (*Carcharhinus melanopterus*) cruises through a school of fish.

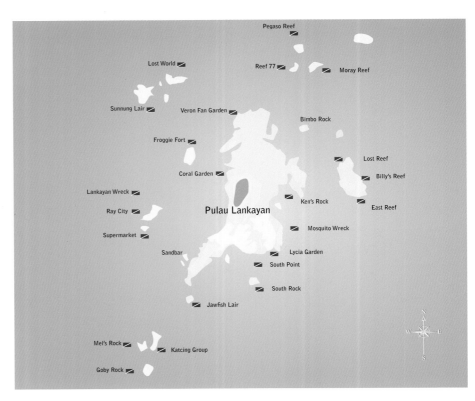

A school of Diamondfish (*Monodactyus argenteus*) take shelter under the jetty.

Soft coral (*Dendronepthya sp.*) growing on a pillar of the jetty.

" *I always enjoy diving under jetties in search of small critters on the seabed, but at Lankayan the abundant schools of fish drew my attention throughout the entire dive as they swirled all around me and the soft coral-covered pilings. In the beautiful, dappled sunlight that trickled down through the wooden planks of the jetty, I wish I could have stayed there shooting forever.* **"**

▲   A trio of Circular Batfish (*Platax orbicularis*) pass under the jetty.

▲ A Reef Needlefish (*Strongylura incisa*) swimming just below the surface, where it catches small fish.

◄ A Dendritic Jawfish (*Opistognathus dendriticus*) sharing its burrow with a White-eyed Moray Eel (*Siderea thyrsoidea*).

► A Dendritic Jawfish (*Opistognathus dendriticus*) removing coral rubble from its burrow.

❝ *This little moray eel appeared from nowhere, then suddenly was embroiled in a short fight with the jawfish, biting each other repeatedly before disappearing down into the jawfish's burrow. When the moray eel reappeared a minute later, the two seemed to have settled their dispute and happily shared the hole together.* ❞

Flashing different colours, the courtship and mating between Broadclub Cuttlefish involves striking visual displays. After mating, the female lays her eggs deep inside a coral head while the male guards the female from predators, and wards off other males. When the small juveniles hatch after 40 days, they hide amongst the coral and rubble on the seabed, often mimicking dead leaves.

▲ A Broadclub Cuttlefish (*Sepia latimanus*) moving over the reef.

▶ A mating pair of Broadclub Cuttlefish (*Sepia latimanus*).

▲ A Leopard Shark (*Stegostoma fasciatum*) rests on the seabed.

Many reef fish such as this Ribbon Eel, display very different colours as juveniles. As they mature, all Ribbon Eels are male, and their skin changes from jet-black to bright, dazzling blue and yellow. When they reach 85cm in length, some males begin to develop female sex organs and change colour once again to entirely yellow.

▶ Portrait of a juvenile Ribbon Eel (*Rhinomuraena quaesita*).

Celebes Sea

▲ The tranquil lagoon of Pulau Sibuan.

Tun Sakaran Marine Park

The Tun Sakaran Marine Park (also known as the Semporna Islands Park) and the Semporna Strait are great places to explore, offering a wide variety of dives and easy access from the nearby fishing town of Semporna on Sabah's east coast. Often overlooked as dive destinations in favour of the more popular islands of Mabul and Sipadan, these locations are in fact well worth taking the time to explore.

The Semporna Strait is fast building a reputation to rival that of the best 'muck' sites in other locations such as Indonesia, and the variety of 'macro' life to be found on a single dive makes the Strait a very special place.

In contrast, the Tun Sakaran Marine Park is the tropical diver's idea of paradise; long sandy beaches, crystal clear water and reefs teeming with colourful fish are the highlights of this protected marine area. Hard coral gardens, sloping reefs and sandy areas provide a variety of habitats that attract a huge diversity of marine life, including plenty of passing pelagic species.

◀ Blue-green Chromis (*Chromis viridis*) in shallow water. Pulau Mantabuan.

◀ ◀ View of Tun Sakaran Marine Park from Pulau Bohey Dulang.

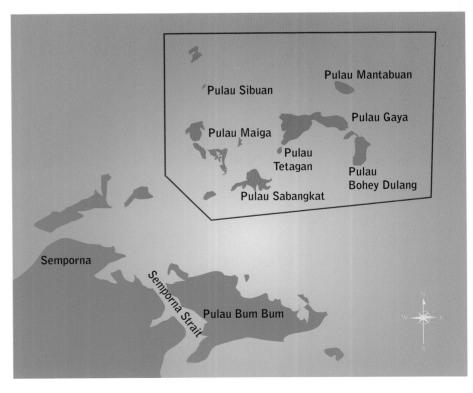

▲ A Giant Clam (*Tridacna squamosa*). Pulau Mantabuan.

▲ Sponge & Black Coral (*Tanacetipathes barbadensas*). Pulau Mantabuan.

▲ Hard coral (*Acropora sp.*) and Bubble Coral (*Plerogyra sinuosa*). Pulau Mantabuan.

Turtles can often be found resting in their favourite spot on a reef. Here they can sleep safe from harm in a rocky crevice, or scratch their shells on sponges to remove algae and parasites.

▶ A Green Turtle (*Chelonia mydas*) nestled amongst sponges and soft coral. Pulau Mantabuan.

▲ Courtship between three Crocodilefish (*Cymbacephalus beauforti*). Pulau Sibuan.

▲ Different colour variations of Giant Frogfish (*Antennarius commersoni*). Pulau Sibuan.

Frogfish are a type of anglerfish that are able to cleverly disguise themselves as sponges or coral. Using a specialized 'lure' attached to its head that mimics small worms or fish and attracts prey, they suddenly open their huge mouths so fast it creates a vacuum and the prey is sucked in. This attack, lasting 6 milliseconds, is the fastest strike of any fish in the world.

▲ Marine File Snake (*Acrochordus granulatus*). Semporna Strait.

This Marine File Snake is adapted to live in coastal areas of mangroves and seagrass. Over time, as this ambush predator lies motionless on the seabed waiting for passing prey, a coating of algae has grown on its body increasing its chances of survival as it blends into its surroundings.

▲ A juvenile Papuan Cuttlefish (*Sepia mestus*). Semporna Strait.

▼ This Halimeda Ghost Pipefish (*Solenostomus halimeda*) mimics the Halimeda seagrass it lives amongst. Semporna Strait.

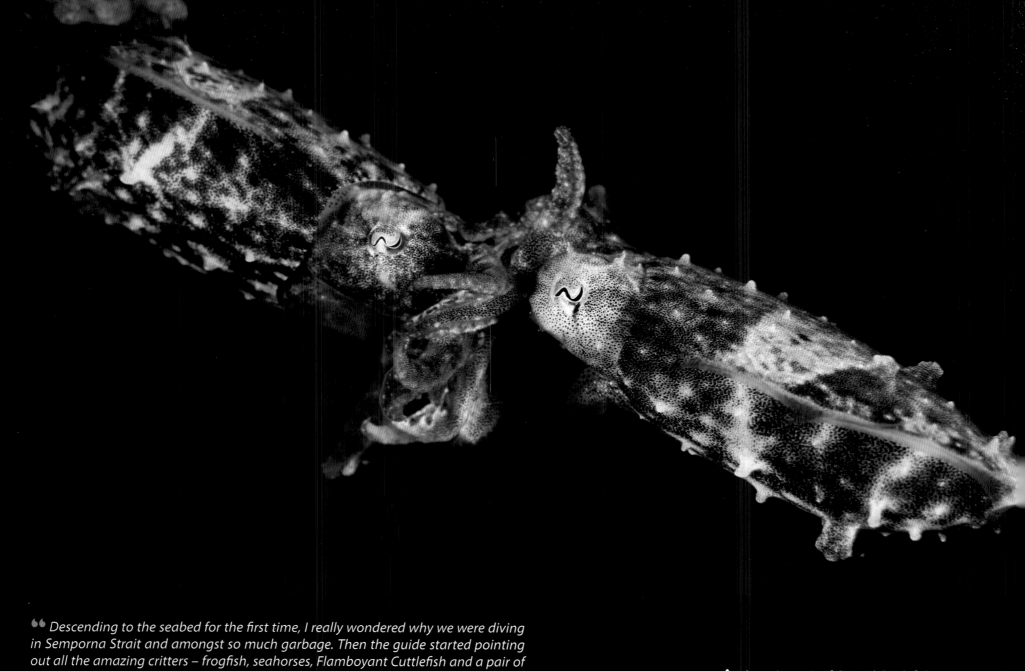

❝ Descending to the seabed for the first time, I really wondered why we were diving in Semporna Strait and amongst so much garbage. Then the guide started pointing out all the amazing critters – frogfish, seahorses, Flamboyant Cuttlefish and a pair of Crinoid Cuttlefish. Ninety minutes later as we ascended I couldn't wait to change my scuba tank and go back down. ❞

▲ A mating pair of Crinoid Cuttlefish (*Sepia sp.*). Semporna Strait.

◀ A pair of Flamboyant Cuttlefish (*Metasepia pfefferi*) prepare to mate. Semporna Strait.

▶ A female Flamboyant Cuttlefish (*Metasepia pfefferi*) laying eggs inside a discarded tin can on the seabed. Semporna Strait.

▲ A courting pair of Picturesque Dragonets (*Synchiropus picturatus*) ready to mate. Semporna Strait.

▲ A juvenile Barramundi (*Cromileptes altivelis*). Semporna Strait.

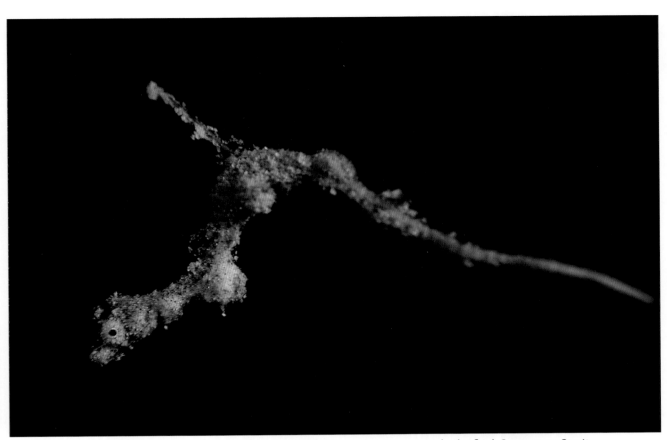

▲ A rare and minute Lembeh Seadragon (*Kyonemichthys rumengani*) is a very lucky find. Semporna Strait.

The alluring pristine corals and colourful reef fish of Sabah are what most divers know and love. However, exploring the sandy 'muck' sites offers endless opportunities to find rare and interesting small animals. Divers expecting to see corals and large fish on this barren landscape will at first be unimpressed, but with keen eyes and "thinking small, and even smaller" a diver will never be bored.

▲ Pulau Mataking Besar.

North Islands

This group of 6 islands, located 30km east of Semporna, includes the well-known Pulau Pom Pom and Pulau Mataking, as well as a few smaller, less familiar locations.

The picturesque islands of Timba Timba and Pandanan are surrounded by pristine coral reefs, whilst wall dives at Mataking and Bohayan offer an array of colourful sea fans, corals and sponges. A very large resident Great Barracuda, accompanied by a school of Big-eye Trevally, can often be encountered whilst diving under the jetty at Mataking and many small 'critters' such as Leaf Scorpionfish, frogfish, Pygmy Seahorses and decorator crabs can be found along the house reef close to a small shipwreck.

Pulau Pom Pom is home to a large number of Green and Hawksbill Turtles and these beautiful animals are often seen feeding and resting on the house reef, alongside schools of Yellow-backed Fusiliers, and numerous different species of nudibranchs, shrimps, and crabs.

◄ A newly-hatched Green Turtle (*Chelonia mydas*) swims out to sea for the first time. Pulau Mataking Besar.

Pulau Pom Pom

New Life
Lobster Wall

Frog Fish Farm
D'wall

Pulau Pandanan
Pulau Mataking Kecil

Treasure Hunt
Mataking Wreck

Nudibranch Town
Sweet Lips Table

Lobster Lair

Pulau Timba-Timba
Stingray City
House Reef
Pulau Mataking Besar

Jalan -Jalan
Nudibranch Heaven

Magic Rock

Aquarium
Coral Garden

Pistol's Paradise
Garden of Eden

Pulau Kalapuan

Divers Delight

Cahaya Way

Pulau Bohayan

Pancang

Lands End

◀ Gorgonian sea fan & diver. Pulau Timba Timba.

▶ Blue-green Chromis (*Chromis viridis*) and other species of small reef fish use the intricate branches of this Acropora coral for shelter. Pulau Mataking Kecil.

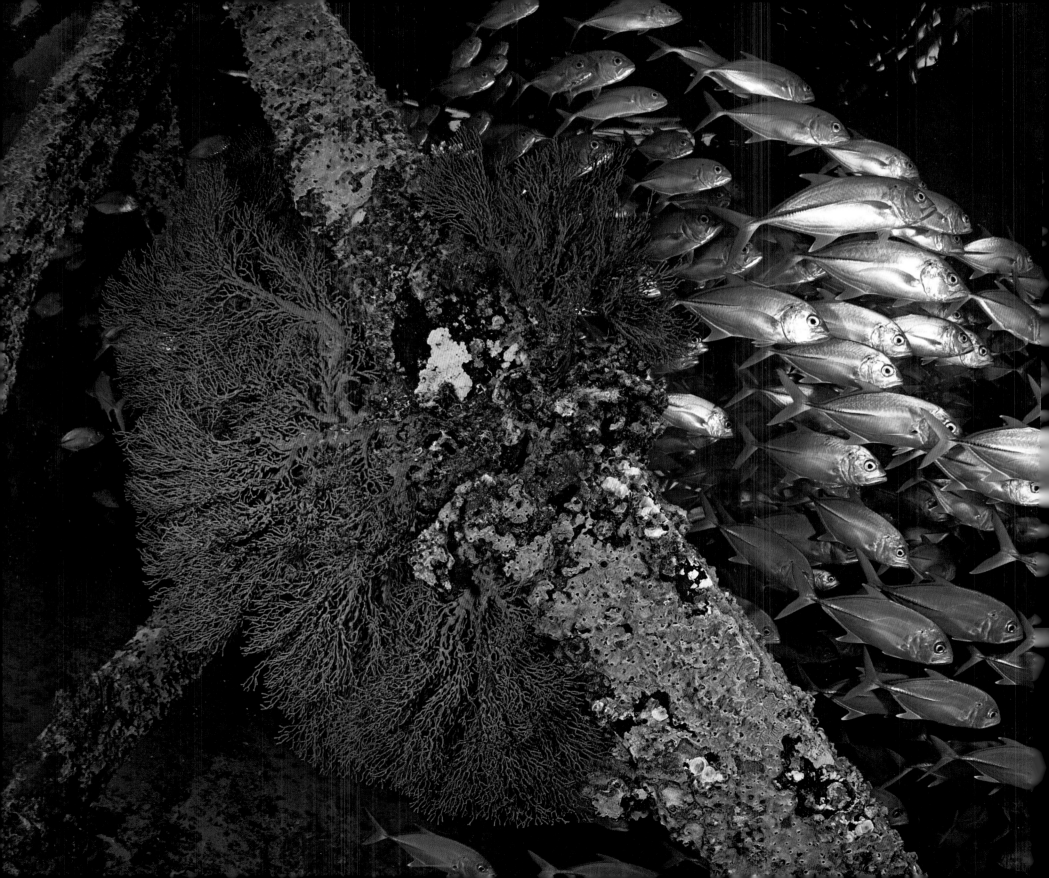

▲ This large, resident Great Barracuda (*Sphyraena barracuda*) nicknamed 'Charlie' can always be seen sheltering under this jetty during daylight hours. Pulau Mataking Besar.

◄ A sea fan and a school of Big-eye Trevally (*Caranx sexfasciatus*) under the jetty. Pulau Mataking Besar.

❝ Each afternoon we would grab our cameras, walk into the sea from the beach, and drift slowly along the house reef searching for, and capturing shots of various reef fish and invertebrates - but it was always nice to know that at anytime we could just swim up from the reef to the resort jetty where the resident Great Barracuda 'Charlie' was always hanging out with schools of Big-eye Trevally. ❞

Small boats are sometimes purposefully sunk in shallow water to create artificial reefs for divers. Within a few years, they become encrusted with corals and sponges, and attract schools of fish that take refuge inside the sunken vessel.

▲ A small school of Glassfish (*Parapriacanthus dispar*) inside a shipwreck. Pulau Mataking Kecil.

▶ A diver explores a small shipwreck. Pulau Mataking Kecil.

TL: Red-lined Flabellina nudibranch (*Flabellina rubrolineata*). Pulau Bohayan.

TR: Anna's Chromodoris nudibranch (*Chromodoris annae*). Pulau Bohayan.

BL: Geometric Chromodoris nudibranch (*Chromodoris geometrica*). Pulau Bohayan.

BM: Linda's flatworm (*Pseudoceros lindae*). Pulau Mataking Besar.

BR: Leopard Chromodoris nudibranch (*Chromodoris leopardus*). Pulau Mataking Besar.

Thousands of species of flatworms and nudibranchs can be found in Sabah's seas, in a kaleidoscope of rich colours and patterns. Many divers love searching for these colourful sea slugs and a few lucky ones are discovering new species.

► A Magnificent Sail-fin Goby (*Flabelligobius sp.*) displays its elaborate dorsal fin during courtship, and also to appear larger than it really is to would-be predators. Pulau Pandanan.

▲ A Sea Cucumber Swimming Crab (*Lisscarcinus obicularis*) on the surface of a Sea Cucumber (*Bohadschia sp.*). Pulau Mataking Besar.

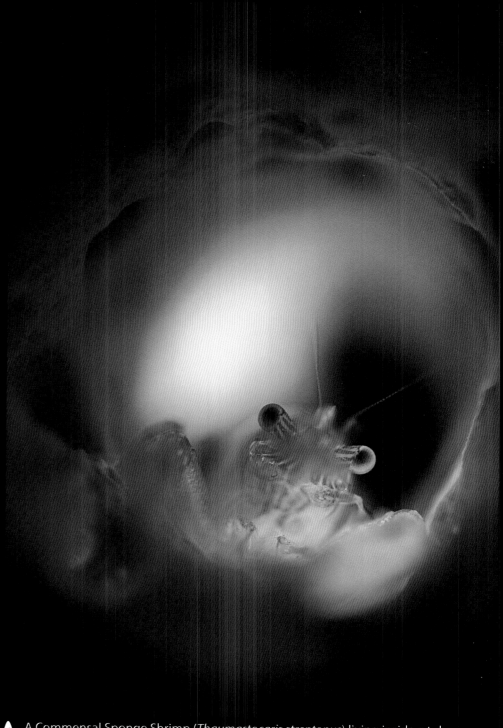

▲ A Commensal Sponge Shrimp (*Thaumastocaris streptopus*) living inside a tube sponge. Pulau Pom Pom.

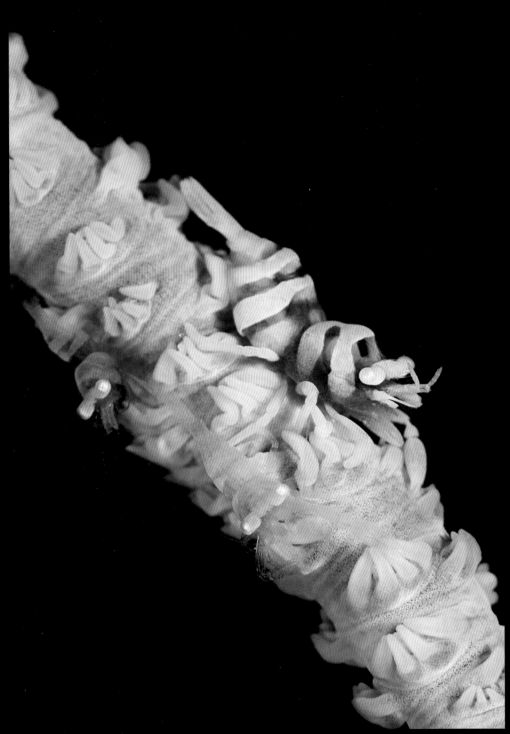

▲ Three Whip Coral Shrimps (*Pontonoides unciger*) on a whip coral. Pulau Mataking.

▲ A Crinoid Shrimp (*Periclimenes amboinensis*) on the frond of a feather star. Pulau Mataking.

A rare Hairy Shrimp (*Phycocaris simulans*) resembles a clump of red algae while resting on the tip of Halimeda seagrass. Pulau Timba Timba.

▲ A tiny Severn's Pygmy Seahorse (*Hippocampus severnsi*), swimming over the sand. Pulau Mataking Besar.

▲ A juvenile Bicolour Parrotfish (*Cetoscarus bicolor*). Pulau Pom Pom.

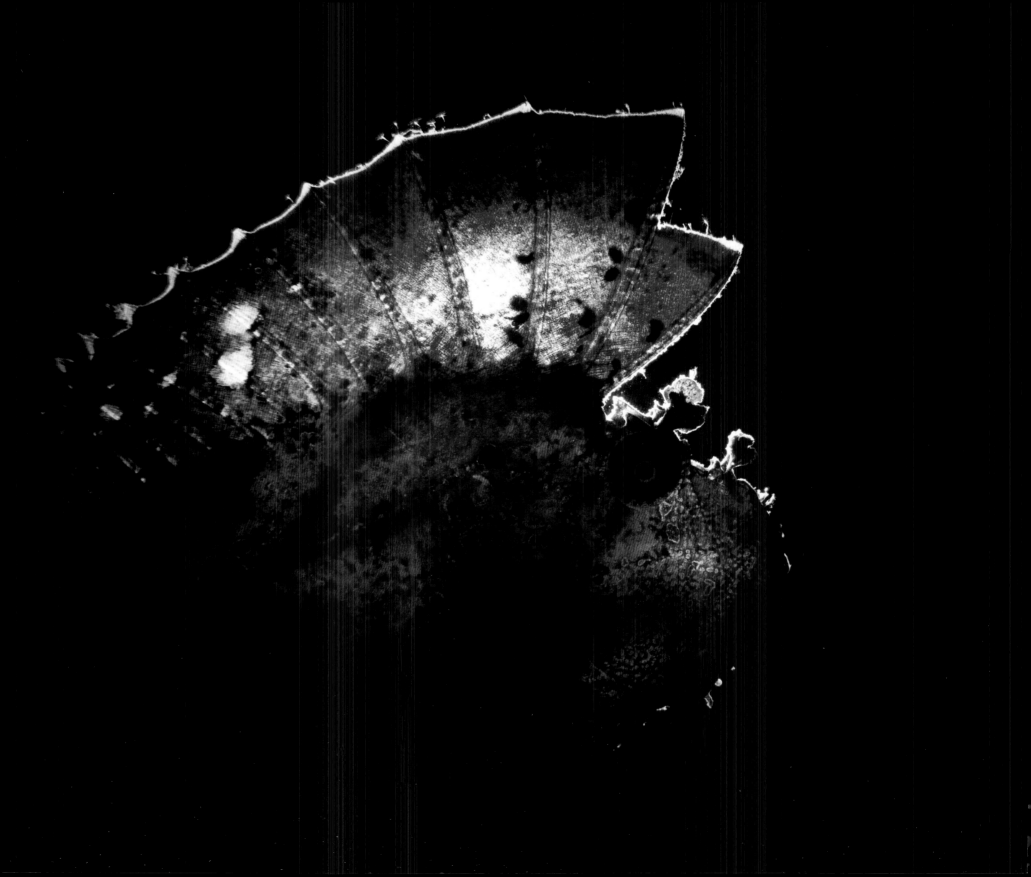

▲ A juvenile Painted Frogfish (*Antennarius pictus*) mimics a toxic Nudibranch with its bright orange spots. Pulau Mataking Besar.

◀ A Leaf Scorpionfish (*Taenionotus triacanthus*). Pulau Mataking Besar.

Leaf Scorpionfish have highly venomous spines on their dorsal, anal, and pelvic fins. Resting on the seabed and coral heads, they mimic dead leaves by swaying their very thin bodies from side to side, and catch smaller fish with their lightning-quick mouths.

▲ A small fishing community on Pulau Ligitan.

Ligitan Reef

Sabah's largest reef system and part of the Sipadan Barrier Reef, the Ligitan reef has three beautiful islands - Pulau Ligitan to the south and Pulau Danawan and Pulau Si Amil to the north. Although the entire edge of the reef can be dived, Si Amil hosts the best dive sites, with shallow sandy slopes to the south-west and a steep wall dropping off to the north-east. The island is the only one in the area with any real topography and its steep hill is covered in dense rainforest.

Like all the islands in the area, Si Amil has some amazing 'macro' life. At first glance, the sandy slopes may appear devoid of life, however Ambon Scorpionfish, Thorny Seahorses, pipefish, frogfish and Cockatoo Waspfish can all be found after some careful inspection of the drifting weed and isolated rocks. The visibility is normally much better along the eastern drop-off facing Alice Channel and, as a result, this area is a good location to search for Pygmy Seahorses in the many gorgonian sea fans, as well as different species of shrimp goby and their blind shrimp partners on the sandy seabed. This spot is also a great location for seeing Devil Rays, with groups of 50+ regularly encountered cruising in the blue water just off the drop-off.

◀ A Porcelain Crab (*Neopetrolisthes oshimai*) & False Clown Anemonefish (*Amphiprion ocellaris*) living together on a sea anemone. Pulau Si Amil.

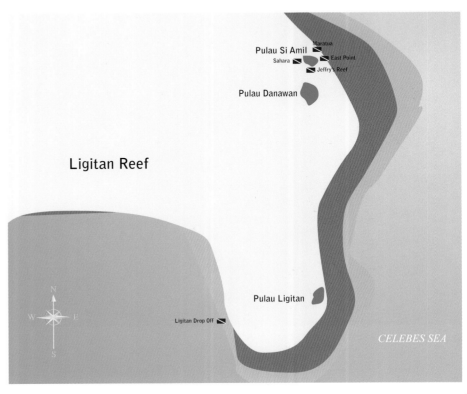

Pulau Si Amil
Maratua
Sahara
East Point.
Jeffry's Reef
Pulau Danawan

Ligitan Reef

Pulau Ligitan
Ligitan Drop Off
CELEBES SEA

▲ Feather stars & soft coral. Pulau Si Amil.

▲ Soft coral (*Dendronepthya sp.*). Pulau Si Amil.

► A yawning Tasselled Scorpionfish (*Scorpaenopsis oxycephala*) & feather stars. Pulau Si Amil.

Pulau Si Amil has very contrasting habitats underwater. To the east the reef drops off steeply to 30m and the walls are covered in colourful sponges and soft corals. To the west the sandy beach slopes gently into the channel between Si Amil and Danawan. At first, this sandy slope may appear empty however, this is where the weird critters like the Cockatoo Waspfish and Robust Ghost Pipefish can be found.

◄ A Thorny Seahorse (*Hippocampus hystrix*) keeps its eyes fixed on the seabed for small shrimps to eat. Pulau Si Amil.

► A Robust Ghost Pipefish (*Solenostomus cyanopterus*) mimics a piece of seagrass as it sways around in the gentle surge. Pulau Si Amil.

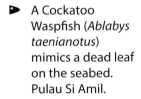

► A Cockatoo Waspfish (*Ablabys taenianotus*) mimics a dead leaf on the seabed. Pulau Si Amil.

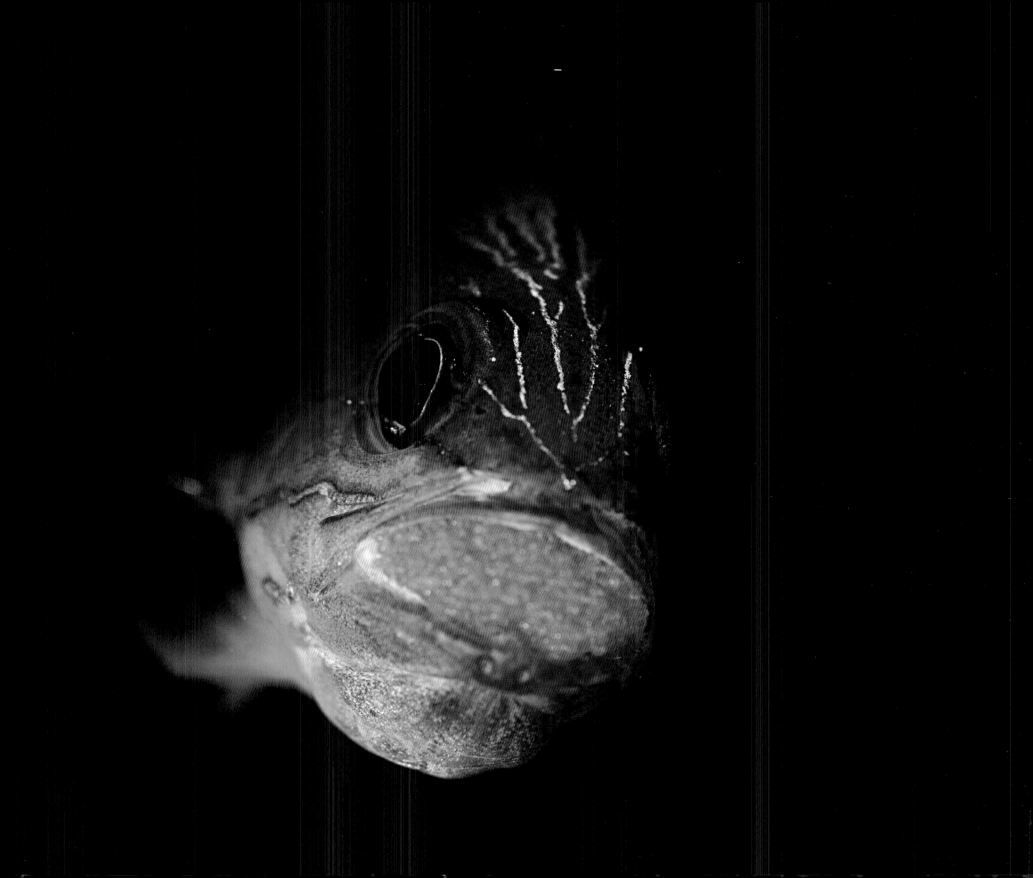

▲ A Tube Anemone Swimming Crab
(*Lissocarcinus laevis*) brooding a cluster
of eggs. Pulau Si Amil.

◄ A Flower Cardinalfish (*Apogon fleurieu*)
mouth-brooding its eggs. Pulau Si Amil.

The majority of fish species mate in a
method known as spawning, meaning
they release free-floating eggs &
sperm into the water column to be
taken away by the current. Some fish,
crabs and shrimp prefer to brood the
eggs and will either have them attached to their bodies, within their
mouths or even in special pouches like
that of seahorses.

▲ A colourful Emperor Shrimp
(*Periclimenes imperator*) living on
the surface of a Sea Cucumber.
Pulau Si Amil.

▶ A Red-gilled Nembrotha
nudibranch (*Nembrotha rutilans*).
Pulau Si Amil.

▲ A Black-headed Sea Snake (*Hydrophis melanocephalus*). Pulau Si Amil.

▲ A Banded Sea Snake (*Laticauda colubrina*). Pulau Si Amil.

There are 62 species of sea snake, distributed from Japan and south-east Asia to the Persian Gulf and Madagascar. All except 5 species live their entire lives at sea, giving birth to live young. However, the Banded Sea Snake is oviparous and must return to land to lay its eggs.

▲ The eye of a Crocodilefish (*Cymbacephalus beauforti*) & Cleaner Shrimp (*Periclimenes magnificus*). Pulau Si Amil.

◄ A Fimbriated Moray Eel (*Gymnothorax fimbriatus*) being cleaned by a Cleaner Shrimp (*Periclimenes sp.*). Pulau Si Amil.

Certain areas on a reef and also some sea anemones serve as important 'cleaning stations' for eels, stingrays and other fish. These can be very productive for underwater photographers as the fish become very relaxed and easier to approach with a camera.

▲ Pulau Mabul with water bungalows.

Pulau Mabul

Pulau Mabul lies 25km south of Semporna and is justifiably renowned for its 'muck' diving on a wide variety of different dive sites, boasting fantastic reefs, and even wall dives. The island's many dive sites offer an impressive diversity of marine life to entice both divers and snorkellers alike, whilst the different dive resorts currently operating on Mabul cater to every diver's budget.

The sandy seabed around the island is home to various species of frogfish and scorpionfish, bizarre-looking seadragons and an abundance of rare and unusual cephalopods such as Flamboyant Cuttlefish and Poison Ocellate, Blue-ringed and Mimic Octopus. Various artificial structures and small wrecks can be seen around Mabul, all of which have become havens for schools of fish, cryptic marine life, and Big-fin Reef Squid that use the structures to shelter their eggs. Divers exploring the reefs can also see many different species of crabs and shrimps, including Mantis Shrimp, Boxer Crabs and the rare and beautiful Harlequin Shrimp. The dive site 'Paradise' is also home to a bed of seagrass, perfect for searching for seahorses and snake eels.

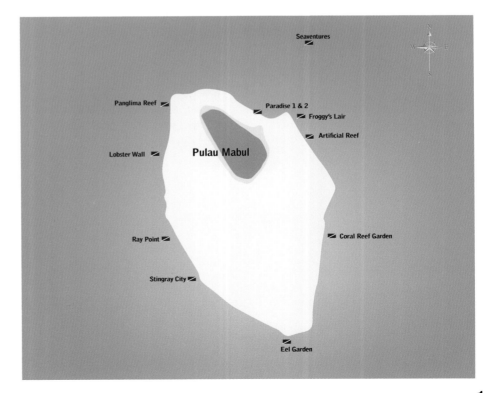

◀ A Common Lionfish (*Pterois volitans*) hunting Robust Silversides (*Atherinomorus lacunosus*) under a jetty.

▲ A school of Indian Snapper (*Lutjanus madras*) on a small wreck below Seaventures.

Sinking old dive boats and constructing artificial reefs has become common practise by a few resorts on Mabul. It's amazing to see how quickly marine life habituates these new homes, from the tiny gobies and blennies to the huge schools of snapper, trevally and even the top predator like the Giant Grouper.

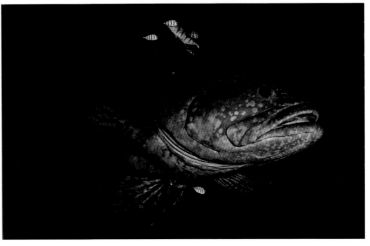

▲ Big-eye Trevally (*Caranx sexfasciatus*) schooling over one of the many large reef structures created by SMART.

▶ Giant Grouper (*Epinephelus lanceolatus*) swimming with Pilot Fish (*Gnathanodon speciosus*).

▲ Big-fin Reef Squid (*Sepioteuthis lessoniana*) laying eggs in the roots of dead palm trees inside a wreck.

◄ Big-fin Reef Squid (*Sepioteuthis lessoniana*) hover above the wreck of a small dive boat.

Waiting patiently, mating pairs of Big-fin Reef Squid take turns to lay eggs amongst the roots of dead palm trees. The male swims around, flashing brightly to draw attention away from its female partner as she lays her eggs one at a time.

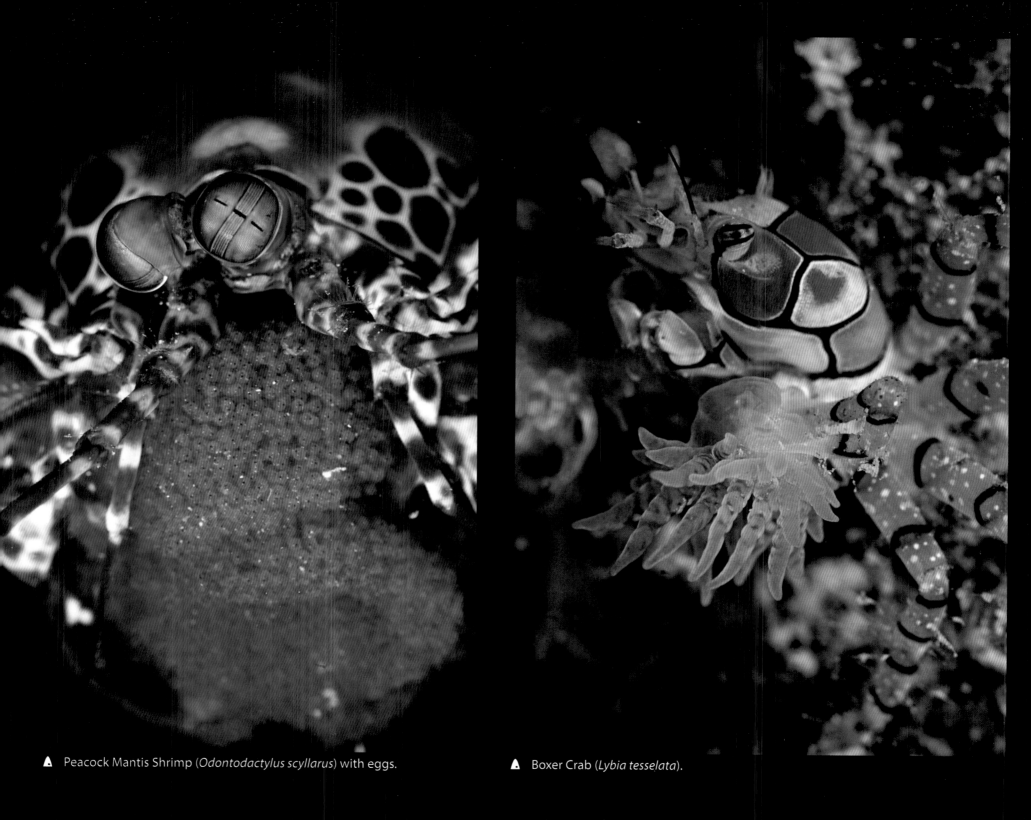

▲ Peacock Mantis Shrimp (*Odontodactylus scyllarus*) with eggs.

▲ Boxer Crab (*Lybia tesselata*).

Shrimp (*Hym*

▲ Flamboyant Cuttlefish (*Metasepia pfefferi*) egg.

❝ *Flamboyant Cuttlefish hatchlings are some of the cutest creatures I've ever seen underwater. As I was shooting them in their eggs I was amazed how they already had the ability to rapidly change colour, and were perfect little miniatures of the adults - a dazzling array of pink, purple and yellow. Seeing them wriggle around inside their egg sac was a wonderful sight, knowing they were soon about to 'pop' and drift away to start their new life in the outside world.* ❞

▲ ▼ A tiny Broadclub Cuttlefish (*Sepia latimanus*) hatching from its egg.

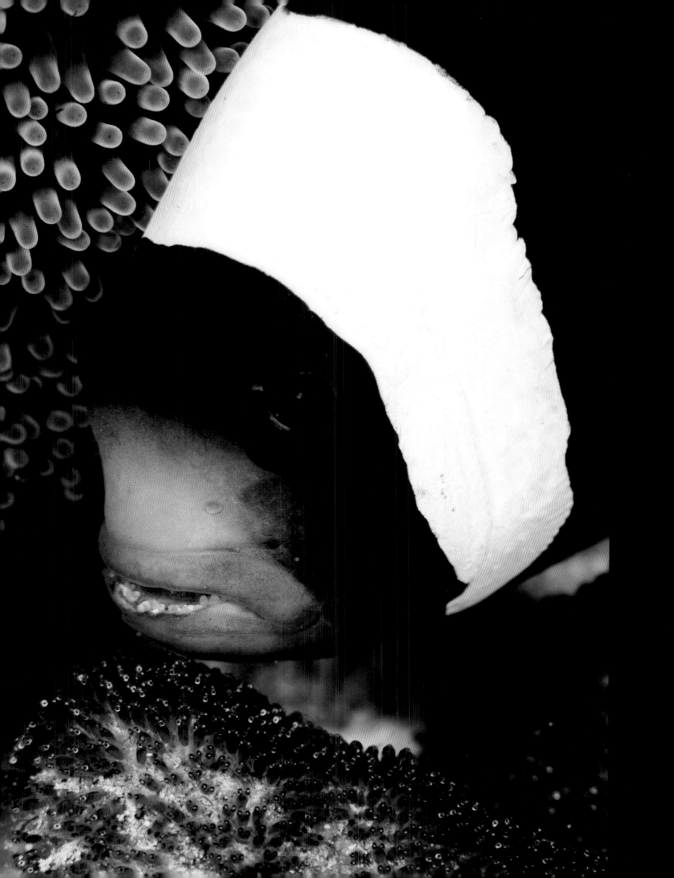

Anemonefish lay their eggs on hard surfaces close to their host anemone, and protect and clean them until they hatch after about 10 days. Juvenile anemonefish are all males, and as they mature some will eventually develop into females.

◄ A Saddleback Anemonefish (*Amphiprion polymnus*) broods its eggs.

► Saddleback Anemonefish (*Amphiprion polymnus*) eggs ready to hatch.

Frogfish and scorpionfish are often seen opening their large, cavernous mouths and yawning. This can be a way of stretching their jaw muscles so they are ready to strike at prey, but more often it is a sign of aggression.

◄ A Giant Frogfish (*Antennarius commersoni*) yawning.

► A Clown Frogfish (*Antennarius maculatus*) yawning.

When the Spanish Dancer nudibranch is disturbed on the seabed by a predator, it will take off and swim into the water column to escape. This mesmerizing animal is so-called because of the undulating movements of its flattened body when it swims, reminiscent of a Spanish flamenco dancer.

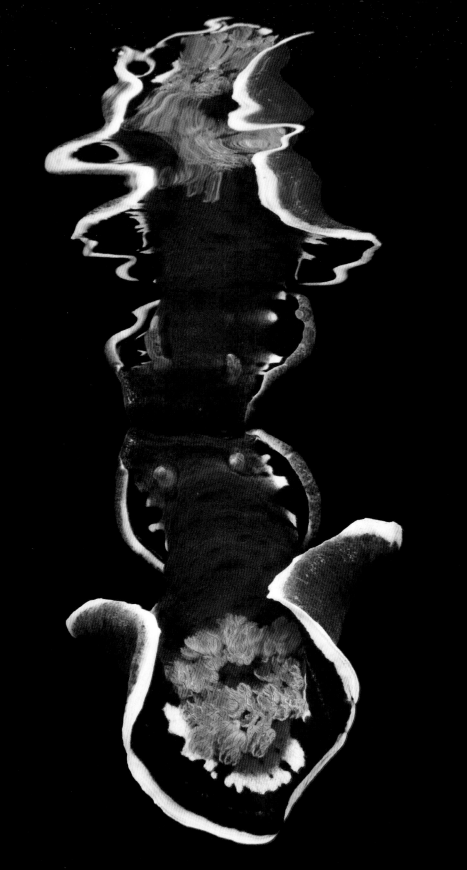

▲ A Napoleon Snake Eel (*Ophichthus bonaparti*)
peers out from its sandy burrow.

◀ A yawning Crocodilefish (*Cymbacephalus
beauforti*).

◀ A Yellow-margin Moray Eel
(*Gymnothorax flavimarginatus*)
being cleaned by a juvenile Blue-
streak Cleaner Wrasse (*Labroides
dimidiatus*).

▶ A Fimbriated Moray Eel
(*Gymnothorax fimbriatus*) & Banded
Cleaner Shrimp (*Stenopus hispidus*).

▲ A Red-lined Flabellina nudibranch (*Flabellina rubrolineata*).

▲ A Commensal Sea Star Shrimp (*Periclimenes soror*) living on the surface of a sea star.

▶ A Pegasus Sea Moth (*Eurypegasus draconis*) walks across the sand.

▲ Sipadan-Kapalai Resort.

Kapalai

Sitting on the edge of the continental shelf, 6km east of Mabul, lies Kapalai. Surrounded by a large, oval-shaped reef, this small sand bar is the eroded remains of an old island once covered by palm trees. There are over 20 dive sites just a few minute's speedboat ride from the resort, and these sites attract divers and underwater photographers drawn by regular sightings of rare and beautiful critters like Blue-ringed Octopus, frogfish, Flamboyant Cuttlefish and ghost pipefish.

A number of resident Green Turtles can always be seen resting on the seabed at sites around Kapalai, and at night feeding on the seagrass beds surrounding the island. Watching these endangered animals feeding in the shallow water, dappled by the lights from the resort, is a wonderful experience.

Diving the house reef reveals a submarine world of large artificial structures and small wrecks, covered with colourful feather stars, sponges and corals, and providing shelter for schools of sweetlips, fusiliers, batfish, as well as a myriad of critters on the sandy seabed.

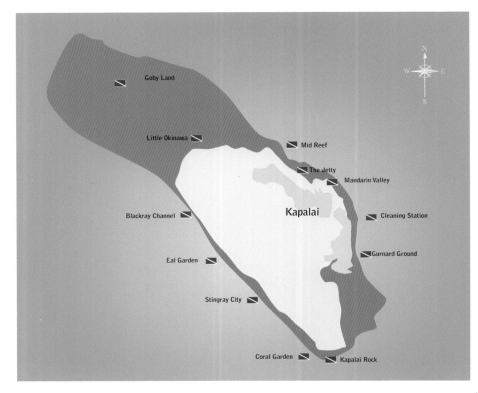

◀ A diver on one of the many wrecks and artificial reefs surrounding Kapalai.

157

▲ Diver & soft coral (*Dendronepthya sp.*) on an artificial structure.

▲ Feather stars under the jetty.

▲ Spotted Sweetlips (*Plectorhinchus chaetodonoides*) shelter under the jetty where they get cleaned by Cleaner Wrasse.

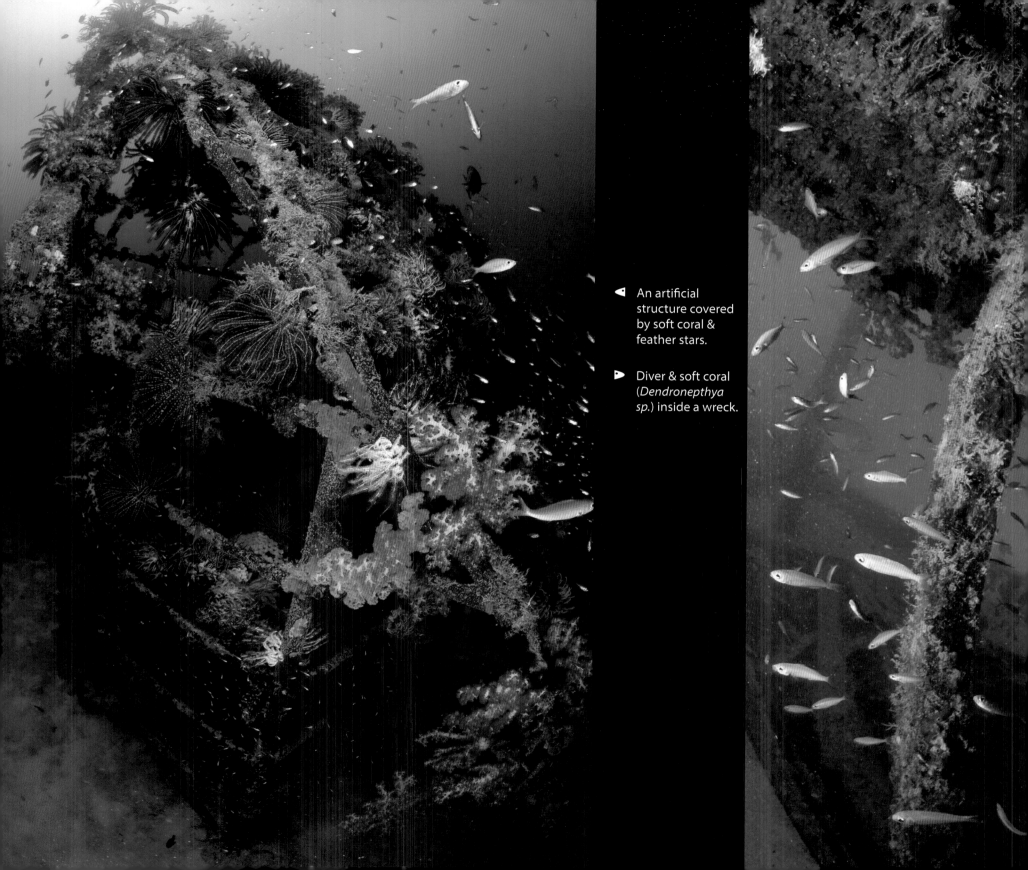

◄ An artificial structure covered by soft coral & feather stars.

▶ Diver & soft coral (*Dendronepthya sp.*) inside a wreck.

A pair of Fire Dartfish (*Nemateleotris magnifica*).

A juvenile Ornate Ghost Pipefish (*Solenostomus paradoxus*).

▲ A pair of Fire Dartfish (*Nemateleotris magnifica*).

▶ A juvenile Ornate Ghost Pipefish (*Solenostomus paradoxus*).

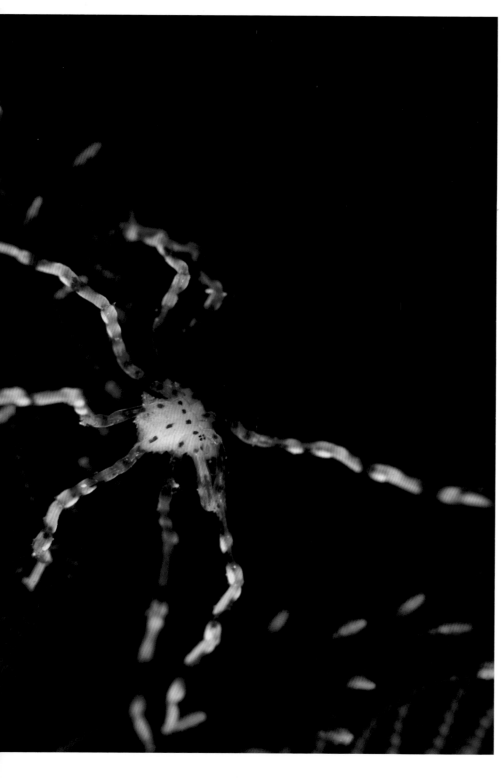

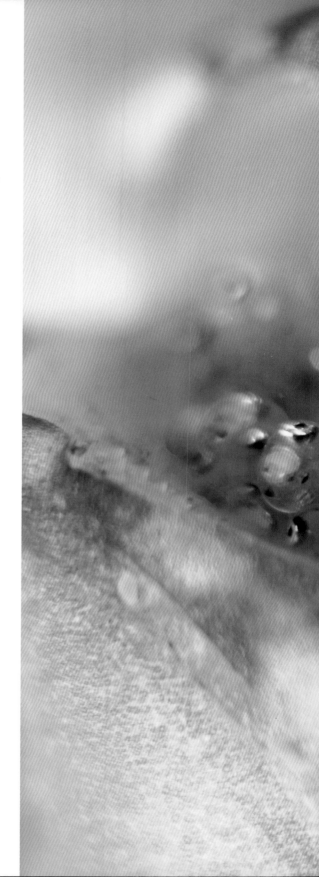

◄ A Sea Spider (*Pseudopallene ambigua*) crawls on the fronds of a feather star safely carrying a clutch of eggs underneath its body.

► A Gold-spectacled Jawfish (*Opistognathus randalli*) mouth-brooding its eggs.

Once a female jawfish's eggs have been fertilized, the male will brood the eggs in its mouth for 8-10 days until they hatch, and during this period he will have no choice but to refrain from feeding.

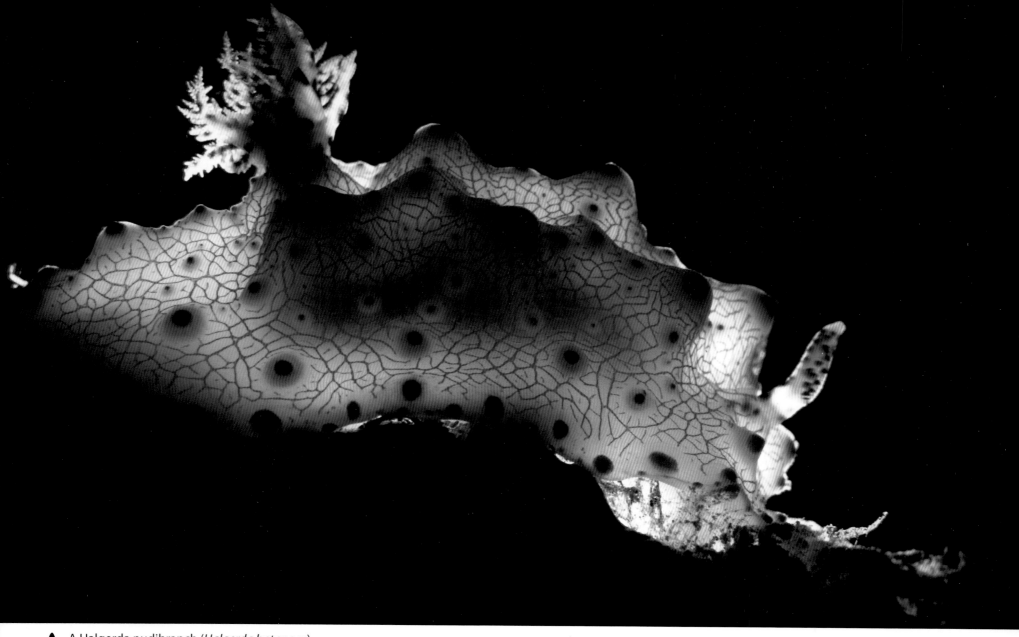

▲ A Halgerda nudibranch (*Halgerda batangas*).

▶ **TL** : Fuchsia flatworm (*Pseudoceros ferrugineus*).

BL : A juvenile Common Egg Cowrie (*Ovula ovum*).

TR : Nembrotha Kubaryana nudibranch (*Nembrotha kubaryana*).

BR : Psychedelic Sagaminopteron nudibranch (*Sagaminopteron psychedelicum*).

The small but deadly Blue-ringed Octopus flashes its blue rings as a warning sign when threatened. One of the world's most deadly marine animals, its bite injects a powerful tetrodotoxin which could kill an adult human within minutes.

◀ A Blue-ringed Octopus (*Hapalochlaena lunulata*) flashes its blue rings as a warning sign.

▶ A Reef Octopus (*Octopus cyanea*) searching for prey at dusk.

" *Octopus are undoubtedly one of my favourite marine animals. Highly intelligent and absolutely fascinating to observe naturally on a reef or sandy seabed, their ability to disguise themselves and become 'invisible' when out in the open is second-to-none, as they can change the colour and texture of their skin to match their surroundings and disappear before my eyes in a matter of seconds. This strategy is used to hide from predators, and also to sneak up on prey – it was incredible to watch this Reef Octopus envelop a patch of reef with its blanket-like body and arms, trapping its prey within.* "

▲ Ijima's Sea Snake (*Embdocephalus ijimae*).

▶ Portrait of a White-mouth Moray Eel (*Gymnothorax meleagris*).

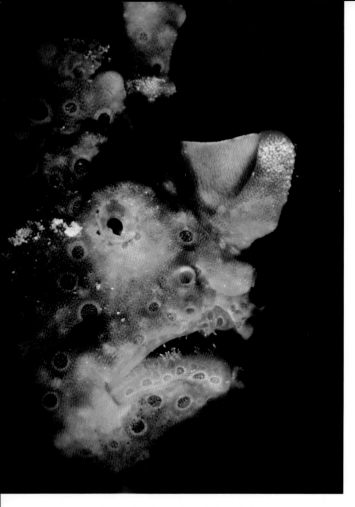

▲ Portrait of a Painted Frogfish
(*Antennarius pictus*).

▶ A diver looks down at a yawning
Giant Frogfish (*Antennarius
commersoni*) on a wreck.

66 *Seeing a frogfish opening its huge,
cavernous mouth and yawn never
ceases to amaze me - it's akin to seeing
a motionless sponge or coral suddenly
come to life. Just when you think its
yawn can't get any bigger, it does,
and it's clear to see how a frogfish can
swallow prey larger than itself!* 99

▲ Green turtles (*Chelonia mydas*) swimming over a shallow reef around the island.

Pulau Sipadan

Consistently voted as one of the top dive destinations in the world, Pulau Sipadan is a must for any passionate diver visiting Sabah. Sipadan is Malaysia's only oceanic island. This tiny speck of land, located 40km south of Semporna, is in fact a needle-like pinnacle of rock and reef surrounded by 600m deep water – a constant source of nutrient-rich upwellings. These nutrients provide the basis for a remarkable food chain that culminates in the many large animals commonly encountered in Sipadan's waters. In recognition of this unique and productive ecosystem, the area is now carefully protected, with limits on the number of divers that can visit every day and a ban on resorts on the island itself.

As you descend into Sipadan's clear waters, the first things that greet you are the sheer walls dropping down into the abyss, the pristine, colourful reefs, the Green and Hawksbill Turtles, too numerous to count, and the dense schools of fusilier, batfish and anthias. Then you notice the intimidating mass of jacks and barracuda, the Napoleon Wrasse and White-tip and Grey Reef Sharks, and your eyes are drawn out into the blue, as tales of Whale Sharks, Manta Rays and Hammerhead Sharks run through your mind. Diving around Sipadan can be a dizzying experience and the sheer number of highlights brings divers back, time and time again.

◄ Only a few meters from the island, the reef drops off 600m down the steep wall.

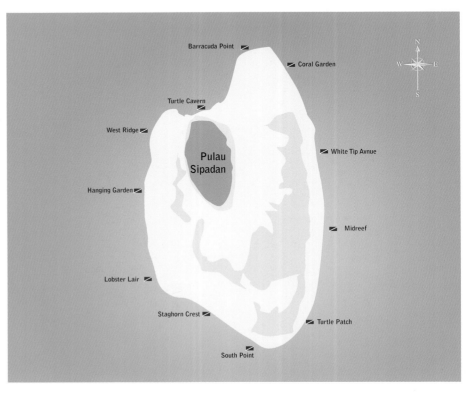

175

◄ Anthias (*Pseudanthias sp.*) swimming in the nutrient-rich water above the coral reef.

▶ A plethora of coral species make up Sipadan's diverse reefs.

Dominant and colourful male anthias have a 'harem' of up to 30 females. If the male dies, the largest and strongest female will change into a male over the course of 2-3 weeks.

Soft coral (*Siphonogorgia godeffroyi*)

Sea fans (*Subergorgia mollis*)

▲ Sea fan (*Semperina sp.*).

▲ A Clown Triggerfish (*Balistoides conspicillum*).

Coral reef fish exhibit a huge variety of striking colours, which can help species recognition during courting and mating. Their colours are in stark contrast to pelagic fish, which are often countershaded with silvery colours to decrease the chances of detection by predators from above and below.

▲ A Yellow-masked Angelfish (*Pomacanthus xanthometopon*).

▲ A male Square-spot Anthias (*Pseudanthias pleurotaenia*).

▲ A fast-moving school of Big-eye
   Trevally (*Caranx sexfasciatus*).

◄ A school of Big-eye Trevally (*Caranx
   sexfasciatus*) swim in the clear blue
   water under a dive boat.

▲ The head of a Chevron Barracuda
(*Sphyraena qenie*).

◀ A school of Chevron Barracuda
(*Sphyraena qenie*) swim over the
pristine, shallow reef.

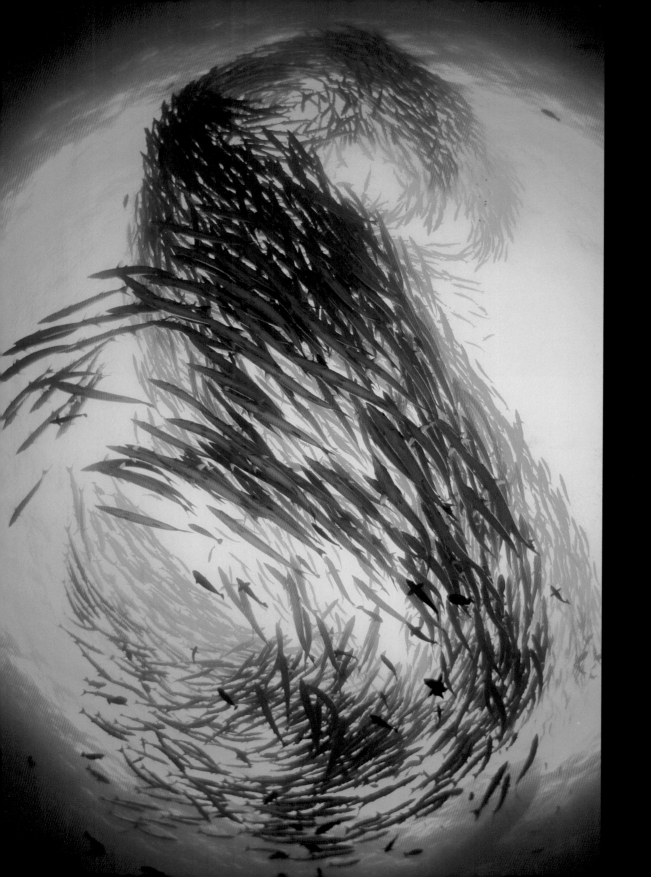

◀ ▶ Schooling 'tornadoes' of Chevron Barracuda (*Sphyraena qenie*).

A huge school of barracuda can form a swirling 'tornado' from the sea's surface down to a depth of 30m. These spectacular schools, which may contain thousands of individuals, will break up at dusk as the barracuda head off to hunt for food, and convene again at dawn.

▲ Boer's Batfish (*Platax boersii*).

▲ Black Snapper (*Macolor niger*).

▲ A freediver (*Ai Futaki*) swims amongst a large school of Bumphead Parrotfish (*Bulbometopon muricatum*) in the shallow lagoon.

▲ A large school of Bumphead Parrotfish (*Bulbometopon muricatum*).

▶ Bumphead Parrotfish (*Bulbometopon muricatum*) excreting sand.

Bumphead Parrotfish have strong beaks to feed on live corals and algae, and a single adult will ingest tons of coral each year which is excreted as white sand. Their feeding activity is important for the production and distribution of coral sand within a reef, and to prevent growing algae from choking coral.

▲ White-tip Reef Shark (*Triaenodon obesus*)
swimming through a school of Big-eye
Trevally (*Caranx sexfasciatus*).

◄ White-tip Reef Sharks (*Triaenodon obesus*)
cruising through a school of Big-eye Trevally
(*Caranx sexfasciatus*) at sunset.

During the day, White-tip Reef Sharks ofte
rest under ledges or on the seabed, an
achieve this by their unique ability to pum
water over their gills. Emerging at dusk, the
scour the reef crevices for fish, crustacean
and octopus. When an unlucky victim
found hiding, several sharks may block a
possible exits and when caught, a feedin
frenzy can occur.

A resting White-tip Reef Shark (*Triaenodon obesus*).

▲ A juvenile Grey Reef Shark (*Carcharhinus amblyrhynchos*) cruises in the deep blue.

▶ A Leopard Shark (*Stegastoma fasciatum*) resting on the seabed, with a Remora (*Echeneis naucrates*) attached to its body.

▲ ◀ Green Turtle (*Chelonia mydas*).

The diet of sea turtles depends on the type of habitat in which they are found. In the open ocean Green Turtles feed on jellyfish, but mainly forage among coastal seagrass beds and eat algae on reefs, which helps to maintain the health of the coral.

▲ ▶ A mating pair of Green Turtles (*Chelonia mydas*).

◀ Mating Green Turtles (*Chelonia mydas*) with a group of chasing males.

❝ *Between dives on a boat just off Sipadan, we heard the huge sigh as a female Green Turtle surfaced to gasp for a breath. This was mating season and we turned to see a pair bobbing calmly at the surface, the male firmly grasped to the female's shell. Grabbing my snorkel gear, I silently entered the water and cautiously made my way over to them. The calm above the waves was a stark contrast to the commotion below as up to seven more males fought, bit and pushed their way to*

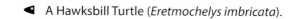
◄ A Hawksbill Turtle (*Eretmochelys imbricata*).

Hawksbill Turtles are mostly found on coral reefs and their diet consists of sponges, soft coral, and algae. Sponges contain toxins which the Hawksbill is immune to and it therefore has less competition for this food source.

▲ A Hawksbill Turtle (*Eretmochelys imbricata*) feeding on soft coral.

Skeletons litter the cave floor of 'Turtle Tomb' which has become the final resting place for many unlucky turtles. After entering the myriad of small passageways at the rear of the large 'Turtle Cavern', for a rest, upon awakening these unfortunate victims eventually lose their way and drown, unable to find an exit to the surface.

◄ A diver in the large opening to 'Turtle Cavern'.

▶ A diver investigates a turtle skeleton inside 'Turtle Tomb'.

▲ Diver explores deeper into the
darkness inside 'Turtle Tomb'.

▶ Turtle skeleton inside
'Turtle Tomb'.

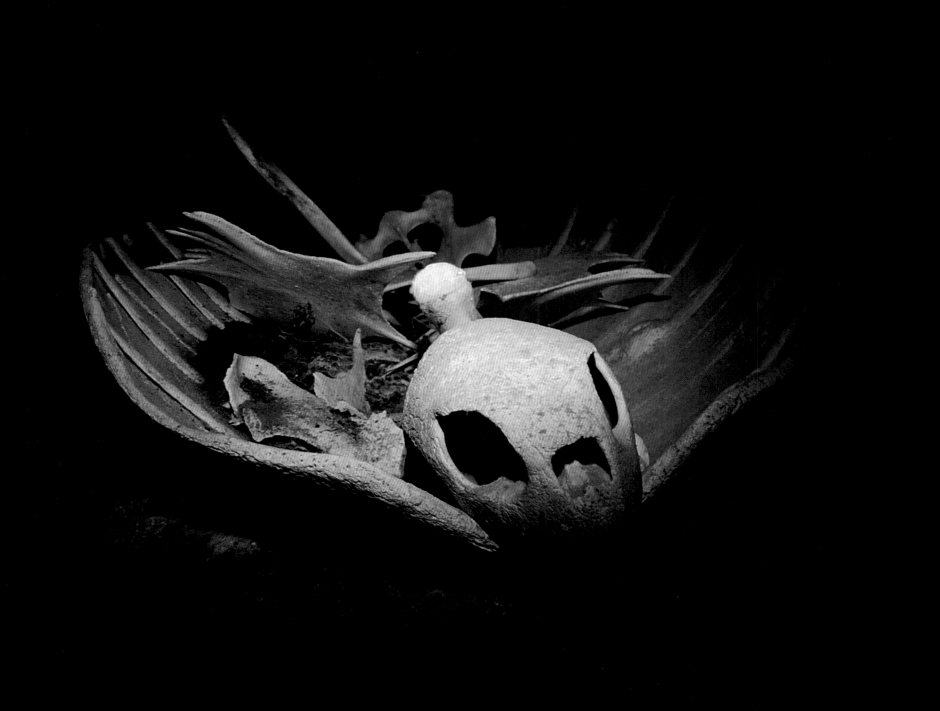

The Future

The marine environment is an enormously valuable resource for mankind. It is utilised for food, protection, employment and recreation, with many many millions of people depending on resources provided by marine and coastal ecosystems for their day-to-day survival. As the world's population and consumption levels increase, threats and pressures on the marine environment are also rising – in fact, the marine world is fast becoming damaged irrevocably.

Sabah's seas face many of the threats now faced by similar habitats around the globe. Population levels in the state continue to rise and with the added pressures brought about by the influx of visiting tourists, extra care must be taken to protect Sabah's marine environment before it is too late. A combination of different threats – over-extraction of resources, cyanide fishing, dynamite fishing, shark finning, mangrove destruction and environmental pollution – all take their toll on Sabah's extremely precious marine resources.

Coral Reefs – The fragile structure of coral reefs make them highly susceptible to damage caused by small changes in the environment. Experts estimate that the world has already lost 19% of its coral reefs, with a further 15% threatened with loss in the next 10–20 years. These losses are due to pollution, destructive fishing practices, climate change and other anthropogenic damage.

▲ Washed up bottles and cans on one of Sabah's beaches.

In tropical waters, the practice of fish bombing or dynamite fishing has destroyed vast areas of coral reef that will take years to recover, if at all. Cyanide fishing for the live reef fish trade continues to wipe out species, upsetting the fragile balance of the ecosystem, and sedimentation and silt from human activities on land are choking the reefs, blocking out available light needed for photosynthesis.

Mangroves and the continental shelf – Inter-tidal habitats such as mangrove forests are being extensively cleared for aquaculture (mainly shrimp farming) and other human developments such as housing or tourism projects. However, mangroves play a very important role in coastal protection, forming a buffer zone between the land and the sea. They are also vitally important breeding grounds for many marine species, often being called marine nurseries because of the amount of young fish, including some species of shark, that take shelter within the mangroves before venturing out into the open water.

▲ The complete destruction to a reef caused by dynamite fishing.

▲ An area of mangroves cleared for new housing developments and shrimp farms.

Further offshore, the seabed is also suffering huge damage from trawlers that use large nets to continually scrape the sea floor, indiscriminately catching anything in their path as they search for a few valuable species, such as shrimps. This practice results in a huge amount of 'worthless' by-catch, which is simply discarded and thrown back into the sea.

Open Ocean – Overfishing is possibly the biggest threat to species found in the open ocean. For instance, commercial fishing vessels fitted with high-tech 'fish-finder' devices strip the seas of huge shoals of fish at an extraordinary rate – at least 70% of the world's fish populations are now considered to be over-exploited by such commercial fisheries. But this is not the only threat. Much of the recent temperature rise attributed to global warming is being absorbed by the seas and according to the recent International Programme on the State of the Oceans (2013), the acidity of the oceans is increasing at a rate without precedent in the last 300 million years. The cause? Burning of fossil fuels and subsequent release of carbon dioxide into the atmosphere, which is then absorbed by the ocean increasing its acidity. Coral reefs are particularly vulnerable to such changes as the acidity dissolves calcium carbonate, the skeletal structure of the reef.

Humans have been partly shielded from the worst effects of global warming by the oceans' ability to absorb carbon dioxide and heat from the atmosphere. This has probably slowed the effects of climate change on land, but the impact on the marine environment is only now beginning to be understood. Nevertheless, despite the current bleak outlook, there is hope amongst experts that trends can be reversed and the marine environment – including Sabah's seas – can be conserved for future generations.

▲ Grouper for sale in a tank in a seafood restaurant.

▲ Grouper being collected by cyanide fishing.

▲ Replanting broken coral on a damaged reef.

The Marine Research Foundation (MRF) also has two long-term projects in Sabah, both focusing on some of Sabah's most charismatic animals – turtles. The first is a population dynamic and growth study of Green Turtles. The majority of information about turtle biology comes from studies of nesting turtles. Instead, the MRF project uses a catch and release method to collect data about foraging juveniles, gathering essential information about a little known part of the life cycle of turtles and helping future management efforts. The second project targets fisheries and promotes the use of a turtle exclusion device (TEDs) in fishing nets. These have no impact on the fishing catch rate of important commercial species but dramatically reduce by-catch of species such as turtles and other large marine animals.

The Semporna Islands Project is a collaborative community and conservation initiative spear-headed by the UK-based Marine Conservation Society (MCS) and Sabah Parks. Its vision is to protect the natural features and rich biodiversity of the Tun Sakaran Marine Park, which covers 35,000 hectares of islands, reefs and sea and is home to almost 3000 people. Promoting the sustainable use of reef resources through alternative livelihood opportunities is a key component to reducing pressures on marine resources, thereby ensuring a better future for those living in and around the Park.

Through synergies between governmental and non-governmental organisations, committed civil society groups and individuals, Sabah's future is indeed looking better. By working together, sharing ideas and strategies and looking at long-term plans as well as immediate actions, positive changes are already being seen.

Large areas of Sabah's seascape have already been gazetted and are now under the management of Sabah Parks, the government agency responsible for protected areas. For example, the Tunku Abdul Rahman Park, Turtle Islands Park, Pulau Tiga Park, Tun Sakaran Marine Park and Sipadan Island Park, collectively cover 57,546 hectares of the state. Meanwhile, at 1.02 million hectares, the proposed Tun Mustapha Park off the northern tip of Borneo, will be the largest marine protected area in Malaysia once it is gazetted in 2015.

The World Wildlife Fund (WWF) has been working in Malaysia for over 40 years. WWF-Malaysia is active in the area known as the Semporna Priority Conservation Area, as well as supporting Sabah Parks in the proposed Tun Mustapha Park in the Kudat-Banggi Priority Conservation Area – both vitally important sites of exceptionally high biodiversity. These two areas boast complex and linked habitats that are home to endangered marine species such as turtles, sharks and Dugongs, as well as supporting hundreds of coastal communities who depend upon marine resources for their livelihoods. WWF-Malaysia's conservation agenda focuses on strengthening management of natural resources by all stakeholders, including local communities, the private sector and government agencies.

▲ A large turtle hatchery in the Turtle Islands protects thousands of turtle eggs from poachers and predators.

▲ A scientist returns a newly tagged turtle to the sea.

The proposed Semporna Shark Sanctuary (SSS) would not only protect sharks, but also other large marine creatures such as Manta and Devil Rays, turtles and Napoleon Wrasse. The aim of the sanctuary is to protect the ecosystem from further damage and provide a safe and secure environment for sharks and other animals, as well as finding alternative livelihoods for the fishermen in the area. Once everyone appreciates Sabah's sharks are worth more far far more alive than dead in a bowl of soup with the establishment of a successful SSS there will be a dramatically marked improvement in the health and wealth of this large area, including Pulau Sipadan, off the east coast of Sabah around Semporna relatively quickly as a direct result.

Reef Check Malaysia has been working on training divers to gather data on the health of the reefs. This data is then used in education progammes for schools, raising community awareness and encouraging wider participation in conservation efforts.

Individual resorts and dive operators also play a significant role in protecting Sabah's seas - the very foundation of their industry – by planting corals and organizing beach and reef clean ups. Another major role, and one that is often underrated, is to help to spread awareness and understanding of the marine environment – the long term key to its survival. Projects such as Mabul Marine Week help to coordinate resorts' efforts, bring scientists and the public together and spread conservation messages to local people and visiting tourists.

Whilst there are many projects trying to make positive changes and conserve Sabah's seas, individuals can also make a valuable difference – think globally, act locally:

- Do not fish or hunt in protected areas
- Do not feed fish in marine parks
- Avoid touching coral, wearing gloves when diving or damaging and harassing marine life
- Leave places as you find them. Although seashells are pretty, they are a vital part of the marine ecosystem and provide a home for many creatures. Do not remove any creature or natural feature from marine parks
- Do not litter
- Miminise your use of plastic bottles and bags.
- Eat seafood from sustainable fisheries
- Get involved with beach and reef clean ups
- Spread the good marine conservation word far and wide!

▼ Special structures provide a stable footing for coral regrowth in badly damaged areas.

Scubazoo Team

Jason Isley has lived in Sabah since 1996, when he helped to create Scubazoo Sdn Bhd. An experienced cameraman and photographer, he has filmed and photographed extensively all over the world. Focusing on his passion for photography and design, Jason is the driving force behind Scubazoo Publications.

Gilbert Woolley, Scubazoo photographer and project manager, has been involved with natural history imagery for the past 17 years as an editor, creative director and photographer. He has worked on countless books during this time and has combined his scientific background with creative photography and design skills in the production of many outstanding recent publications.

Scubazoo photographer **Christian Loader** joined the team in 2007, filming & photographing the marine environment around south-east Asia, including long-term assignments in the Maldives and Indonesia. After turning his attention to photography, Christian's images have won many international awards.

Key: T-Top, B-Bottom, M-Middle, L-Left, R-Right.

Jason Isley: 2-3, 4-5, 11, 12, 16-17, 18, 19, 20, 21, 22, 23, 24(T)(B), 25, 26, 30, 31, 32, 33, 34(M)(R), 35, 36, 38(T)(B), 39, 41, 48, 50, 51, 52, 53, 54(L)(R), 55, 56(T)(B), 58, 59, 60(L)(R), 61, 62(R), 64(B), 65, 66, 67, 68-69, 79, 80, 81, 82, 83, 86, 87, 88, 93, 94(M)(R), 95, 96, 97(L)(M)(R), 98, 99(T)(B), 100, 101(T), 103(L)(R), 107, 120, 122(L)(R), 123, 124, 125(T)(B), 126, 127, 128, 129, 130, 131, 132, 133, 134, 135, 136, 137(T)(B), 138, 139, 140(L)(R), 141(L)(R), 142, 144, 145, 146, 147, 148, 149, 150, 151, 152, 153, 154(B), 157, 158(L), 174, 175, 176, 177, 178(R), 179, 180, 181(L)(R), 183, 184, 185, 186, 187, 188, 189, 190, 191(T)(B), 192, 193, 194, 195(T), 196, 197, 200, 201, 202, 203, 204, 205, 206(T), 207(T), 209(BR), 220, Inside back cover.

Gilbert Woolley: Front cover, 26, 27, 34(L), 37(L)(R), 40, 42, 44, 45, 49, 94(L), 101(BL)(BM)(BR), 102, 104, 106, 110, 112(BM)(BR), 113, 115(L)(R), 143(T)(BL)(BM)(BR), 154(T), 155, 162, 164, 165, 178(L), 182, 198(T)(B), 199, 207(BL), 208(BR), 209(TL).

Christian Loader: Inside front cover, 13(TL)(R), 14, 15(T)(B), 43, 46(T)(B), 47, 70, 71, 72, 73, 74, 75, 76, 77, 78, 84, 85, 89, 90-91, 92, 105, 108, 109, 111, 112(TL)(TR)(BL), 114(L)(R), 116, 117(L)(R), 118, 119, 121, 156, 158(R), 159, 160, 161, 166, 167(TL)(TR)(BL)(BR), 168, 169, 170, 171, 172, 173, 206(BL), 208(TL).

Roger Munns: 9, 29, 207(BR).

Adam Broadbent: 57, 62(L), 63, 64(T), 163, 195(B).

Richard Swann: 28.

OTHER SCUBAZOO BOOKS

Acknowledgements

Having been based in Sabah for 16 years Scubazoo have an extensive knowledge of the diving locations and have also gathered an enormous library of underwater images. However when planning this book we felt the need to capture the latest images from each location and therefore the support from various resorts and dive operators was a necessity to make that happen.

The photographic shoots were spread over an entire year and many people assisted in making them all completely successful.

So, in no particular order, we would like to thank the following:

Chief Minister's Office, Sabah	Datuk Seri Panglima Musa Haji Aman
Ministry of Tourism, Culture & Environment, Sabah	Datuk Masidi Manjun & William Baya
Sabah Tourism Board	Datuk Irene Benggon Charuruks & Hana Harun
Shangri La Hotels & Resorts	
Scuba Junkie	Ric Owen, Tino Herrmann, Rohan Perkins and the special guidance of Rowan Coombe
Seaventures Tours & Travel	Suzette Harris
Sipadan-Mabul Resort / SMART	Robert Lo, Michelle Teo and the amazing cave guidance of Patrick Chong
Pulau Tiga Resort	Charles Wembley Mogindol & Brenda Yandaman
Diverse Borneo	Mark Hedger
Borneo Divers & Sea Sports	Theresa Tham & Jason Wong
Downbelow Marine & Wildlife Adventures	Richard & Joanne Swann
The Reef Dive Resort / GTS Travel Services	Carol Teh
Traverse Tours / Mari Mari Dive Centre	Octavius Asaad & Lynn Li
Layang Layang Island Resort / Avillion	Lawrence Lee
Sipadan Scuba	Jerry Reichart
Sipadan Pom Pom Resort & Tours	Peter Loong, Jessie Cheam & Ron P Freddy Bagang
WWF Malaysia	Robecca Jumin & Irwanshah Mustapa

Thanks to Neville Kippenberger for his critter-spotting skills in TARP.

For all their advice and help with the printing: **PNMB** / Izham Bin Yusoff.

Our choice of camera equipment has always been Nikon and the underwater housings of choice are Nauticam. Nauticam housings have an amazing design and incredible durability – they have to when Scubazoo photographers get their hands on them! Many thanks to Edward Lai, Phoebe Lu & Jacqueline Lai.

Special thanks to Scubacam (Singapore) for all the support with equipment and the crazy gadgets: David Cheung & Sanah Zakaria.

Inon strobes are supported as usual by Ultralite Control Systems: Terry Schuller and Dave Reid.

When undertaking long photographic shoots and extended periods of time underwater, our comfort is extremely important and for that reason we would like to thank the continuous support from Dive Rite, Pinnacle and Seventenths.

All online films were shot using Sony cameras and these are kept dry by Gates Underwater Products, the most reliable and durable underwater housings on the market. Many thanks for the continuous support: John Ellerbrock & Pamela Mazey Mert.

USEFUL LINKS

Sabah Parks — www.sabahparks.org.my
WWF-Malaysia — www.wwf.org.my
Semporna Islands Project — www.sempornaislandsproject.com
Semporna Shark Sanctuary — www.borneoconservancy.org/our-work/sharks
Marine Research Foundation — www.mrf-asia.org
Reef Check Malaysia — www.reefcheck.org.my
International Program on the State of the Oceans — www.stateoftheocean.org
Marine Conservation Society — www.mcsuk.org

SABAH TOURISM BOARD

Ministry of Tourism Development,
Environment & Technology,
Sabah, Malaysia.

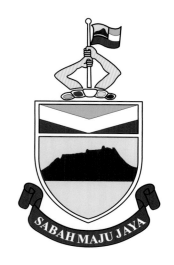

Ministry of Tourism Development, Environment and Technology
5, 6, 7 Floor, Block A, (Alliance Bank Towers),
Wisma Tun Fuad Stephens, 88300 Kota Kinabalu,
Sabah, Malaysia.
Tel: +60 88 253666
Fax: +60 88 236005
Website: www.sabahtourism.net/sc/kepkas/

Sabah Tourism Board
51 Jalan Gaya, 88000 Kota Kinabalu,
Sabah, Malaysia
Tel: +60 88 212121
Fax: + 60 88 212075
Email: info@sabahtourism.com
Website: www.sabahtourism.com

Shangri-La's

Tanjung Aru Resort & Spa
KOTA KINABALU

No. 20 Jalan Aru, Kota Kinabalu, Sabah,
88100, Malaysia
Tel: +60 88 327 888
Fax: +60 88 327 878

Shangri-La's

Rasa Ria Resort
KOTA KINABALU

Pantai Dalit Beach, Tuaran,
Sabah, 89208, Malaysia
Tel: +60 88 797 888
Fax: +60 88 792 777

www.shangri-la.com

SCUBA JUNKIE

Semporna HQ: Lot 35-42, Semporna Seafront, 91308 Semporna.
Kota Kinabalu: Scuba Junkie, G23, Wisma Sabah, Kota Kinabalu.
Island: Mabul Beach Resort, Mabul Island, Sabah.

Tel: +60 88 255 816, +60 89 785 372
Fax: +60 88 250 049
Email: info@scuba-junkie.com
WebSite: www.scuba-junkie.com
www.scubajunkiekk.com

SEAVENTURES TOURS & TRAVEL SDN. BHD.

Room 422-424, 4th Floor
Wisma Sabah, Jalan Tun Razak
88000 Kota Kinabalu, Sabah, Malaysia

Tel : +60 88 261669/251 669
Fax : +60 88 251 667
Email: info@seaventuresdive.com
Website: www.seaventuresdive.com

SIPADAN-MABUL RESORT (SABAH) SDN. BHD.

Lot A-1-G, Block A, Signature Office
KK Times Square, Off Coastal Highway
88100 Kota Kinabalu, Sabah, Malaysia.

Tel No: +60 88 486389
Fax No: +60 88 486628
Email: mabul@po.jaring.my, mabul@streamyx.com
WebSite: www.sipadanmabulresort.com,
www.mabulwaterbungalows.com

PULAU TIGA RESORT

(owned by SIPADAN DIVE CENTRE SDN. BHD (co. no. 236538-X, KKKP 2372)
Office Address: Lot A1026, 10th Flr Wisma Merdeka,
Mailbox No. A236, Jln. Tun Razak,
88000 Kota Kinabalu, Sabah, MALAYSIA

Tel: +6 088 240584
Fax: +6 088 240415
Website : www.sdclodges.com

Pulau Tiga Resort (Located at Pulau Tiga, Kuala Penyu)
Facebook: www.facebook.com/pulautigaresort

DIVERSE BORNEO SDN BHD

Lot G30, Ground Floor,, Wisma Sabah, Jalan Tun Fuad Stephen, 88000
Kota Kinabalu, Sabah, Malaysia

Email : info@diverse-borneo.com
Phone : +60 12 8381630
Facebook: 1diverseborneo
Twitter Instagram : diverseborneo
Website : www.diverse-borneo.com

BORNEO DIVERS AND SEA SPORTS (SABAH) SDN BHD

9th Floor, Menara Jubili,
53 Jalan Gaya, 88000,
Kota Kinabalu, Sabah,
Malaysia.

Tel : +60 88 222 226
Fax: +60 88 221 550
Email: information@borneodivers.info
Facebook: www.facebook.com/BorneoDiversMabulResort
Website : www.borneodivers.net

DOWN BELOW SDN BHD

KK Times Square
Block L, 5th Floor, Lot 67 & 68
Kota Kinabalu 88100
Sabah, Borneo, Malaysia

Email: info@divedownbelow.com
Hotline 1: +60 12 866 1935
Hotline 2: +60 12 867 7375
Fax: +60 88 485 300
Website: www.divedownbelow.com

GTS TRAVEL SERVICE SDN BHD (CO. NO. 52785U)

(Licensed Tour Operator No: KKKP/PL: 1347)
Office: TB 212, Jalan Bunga, Fajar Complex,
91000, Tawau, Sabah, Malaysia.

Tel. No: +60 89 770022 (Reservation)
Fax No: +60 89 770023
Email: sales@mataking.com
Website: www.mataking.com
(Sales Agent for The Reef Dive Resort and Tours Sdn Bhd @ Mataking Resort)

TRAVERSE TOURS SDN BHD (KKKP3505)

Lot 215, 2nd Floor , Wisma Sabah,
Jalan Tun Fuad Stephen, 88100 Kota Kinabalu

Tel: +60 88 260511
Fax: +60 88 260533
Website : www.mantananiisland.com
www.riverbug.asia

LAYANG LAYANG ISLAND RESORT SDN BHD

(Kuala Lumpur Sales & Reservation Office)

Block A, Ground Floor, A-0-3,
Megan Avenue II, 12, Jalan Yap Kwan Seng,
50450 Kuala Lumpur, West Malaysia.

Tel: +6 03 21702184
Fax: +6 03 27309959
Email: res@avillionlayanglayang.com
Website: www.avillionlayanglayang.com

SIPADAN SCUBA

Lot: B7-B8, Ground Floor,
Semporna Seafront Resort Township,
91308 Semporna, Sabah, Malaysia

Booking Number: +6 (089) 919128 / 919148 / 784788
Fax Number: +6 (089) 768531
E-Mail: sipadanonline@gmail.com
Website: www.sipadanscuba.com
Online booking: www.sipadanonline.com
SKYPE: sipadanscuba

SIPADAN POM POM RESORT & TOURS SDN BHD

A-2-1, Karamunsing Capital,
Lorong Kapital, Block A, 2nd Floor,
88000 Kota Kinabalu, Sabah, Malaysia

Tel: +60 88 484 083/ 60 88 484 093
Fax: +60 88 484 098
Urgent Contact/Booking
Tel: +60 16 815 9979 /+60 13 883 3128
Email: info@pompomisland.com
Website: www.pompomisland.com

Index

▶ ▶ Freediver (*Ai Futaki*) and Green Turtle (*Chelonia mydas*), Sipadan.

▶ ▶ Freediver (*Ai Futaki*) and Green Turtle
(*Chelonia mydas*), Sipadan.